Husband Hunting

How to Win at the Mating Game

Jane F. Carpineto, M.S.W.

A Fireside Book
Published by Simon & Schuster, Inc.
New York

Library of Congress Cataloging in Publication Data
Carpineto, Jane.
  Husband hunting.

  "A Fireside book."
  1. Single women—United States.   2. Mate selection—
United States.   3. Interpersonal relations.   I. Title.
HQ800.4.U6C38   1986   646.7'7   86-1944
ISBN: 0-671-60389-2

To Joe, Amy, and Julie
and Antoinette and Joseph Carpineto, Sr.

Acknowledgments

There are many people to thank for their help with this book: Suzanne Wetlaufer, the Associated Press reporter whose feature article made the book possible. Susan Victor, my editor, who believed I could do it and taught me invaluable lessons along the way; Helen Rees, my agent, surely the busiest woman in Boston, yet she never forgets to call or answer a message; my friends Emily and Tom Lamont, Rita and Harry Pothoulakis, Kate Salter, and June Wolff for celebrating with me, and Elliot Klitzman and Linda and Bill Green for both celebrating and counseling; my mentors and friends Sharon Goldsmith, Janice Steil, Bunny and Fred Duhl, Eugene Smith, Ann and Alvin Poussaint, Jessica Lipnack, and Jeff Stamps; my own extended family, east and west; my adult-education network, Paul Fishman, Dale Koppel, and Elsa Galston; my ever-faithful typists, Meg Baer and Cyndee Schnyder; and all of my students and clients.

Special thanks to Elinor Thomas, Kathleen Daley, Sharon Evans, and Colquitt Meacham; my husband, Joe, because he reshuffled his life to make the book easier for me to write and was always the captain of the cheering squad; my daughters, Amy and Julie, who, with a graciousness and good humor uncharacteristic of their age group, tolerated a certain amount of neglect for the sake of "Mom's book!"

Contents

Introduction   9

1 Dispelling the Myths   11

2 The Presenting of Me—Am I Who I Say I Am?   26

3 If I'm O.K., Who's O.K. for Me?   44

4 How to Get Mentally Ready to Meet Mr. Right   59

5 Where Do I Go to Find Mr. Right?   72

6 Building Networks   85

7 How to Be Your Own Worst Enemy in Love: The Seven Most Common Love Traps   95

8 Six Ways to Make the Search Pay Off   111

9 How Do I Know When I've Found Him?   123

Epilogue   135

Introduction

My life, like everybody else's, has had high and low points, and scattered in between have been a few "peak" experiences—times of unparalleled joy. From my mid-life station, I can look back and count six peaks. The first came when I set foot on another continent at the age of 22—at last the long-awaited journey to foreign lands. The second came when I was 31 and had met the man who was to become my husband—the culmination of a few years of active and adventurous looking. The third and fourth were the births of our two daughters, whose arrivals were the more eagerly anticipated because I was well into my 30s when I delivered them. The fifth and sixth occurred in my 47th year of life, when I had my first glimpse of China, a country I had longed to see for many years, and some months later when the opportunity to write this book arose, fulfilling a dream that I had entertained secretly since childhood.

It was the second peak experience, meeting my husband, that became the seed which germinated into the sixth peak—this book. Several years ago, I was a student in a creative-writing class for which there was an assignment to write a part of an autobiography. My vignette was about the time in my life when I had been looking for a husband and how I had eventually found him. The feedback from the teacher and my classmates was as encouraging as it was provocative. "Women need to learn the lessons about men that your own story conveys," they said. Never one to ignore a challenge, I responded by offering classes in adult-education programs to single people on the subject of mating. It was a new idea, and in the beginning they were sparsely attended and overwhelmingly female. Now, more than five years later, they are popular with both sexes, all ages, and a variety of races and ethnic groups. By the time I set about writing this book I had talked with and listened to hundreds of single men and women.

As an author, I have chosen to speak primarily to women, not only because I am one, but also because women seem to experience more difficulty than men in wending their way through the mating maze. The single women I've met have repeatedly asked the same questions which have now become theme songs in my head: Are my beliefs about men true or false? Am I O.K.? Where are the good men? Where do I go to meet them? What am I doing wrong? How do I know *he's* O.K.? What is "love," anyway? Here, as I do in my classes, I attempt to answer these questions.

I hope this book carries another message to women, one that is not in answer to a specific question: To reach the peaks, you first have to travel through the hills and the valleys. It should be an adventure. So if finding a loving husband would represent a joyful "peak" for you, then don't lose sight of it. We'll travel toward it, if you will follow me.

Jane Carpineto
Newton, Massachusetts

CHAPTER 1

Dispelling the Myths

There are almost as many doomsayers in our midst as there are single people. You know the kind I mean. Remember that last singles function that you mustered up enough courage and cautious anticipation to attend? Just inside the door, your heart sank as you gazed at a sea of female faces interspersed occasionally with a rarer species—men. Having gone to the trouble to get there, you made a quick mental decision to stay and make the best of it. With waning enthusiasm, you went to get a drink and there she was—Ms. Doomsayer. She was nice looking and about your age. You weren't long into a conversation before her litany began. She's tried everything to meet a man, and it seems as if this time she came here for the sole purpose of telling you that "*nothing works.*" She's been everywhere and she knows that there aren't any good men left. You've met her type before—at the office, at your health club, at community meetings, or at other parties. In fact, you know her well because *there's a little bit of her inside of you.*

Now I've brought you willingly or not to a crucial crossroad. If you decide to let the doomsayer in you get the upper hand, *you're letting go* of both the joy and the reward of husband hunting. Your first and most important decision, *if you're really looking for a mate*, is to squelch your own voice of doom. Contrary to what our doomsayers tell us, there are a lot of things you can do to find Mr. Right. But before you embark on this adventurous journey, you'll have to unpack and repack your suitcase.

First, let's unpack all the myths that you've been carrying around. They're too cumbersome and ill-suited to the climatic fluctuation that will occur in your travels.

Myths About Marriage

Myth #1: Marriage is for Everyone.

It is true that most single people prefer marriage to singledom. In their representative study of single people in the United States, *Singles—The New Americans*, Jacqueline Simenauer and David Carroll found that only one-third of single men and one-fifth of single women remain single because they prefer the single lifestyle. The overwhelming majority of both men and women interviewed planned to marry or remarry.*

Here, I am not addressing those women who know

---

* Jacqueline Simenauer and David Carroll, *Singles—The New Americans* (New York: Simon and Schuster, 1982), p. 322.

that they desire to remain single, rather I am speaking to those who might *unknowingly* prefer the single life. I don't need to be convinced that there are women who might relish the total freedom to do whatever they wanted without the constraints that sharing their lives with a partner would entail, but I am less convinced that these women always know who they are.

There are some clues to help you identify yourselves. We've all had doubts about our abilities as marriage partners, but if you've had persistent, nagging doubts and trouble visualizing yourself married, *STOP* and take a hard second look before proceeding. Likewise, if you've frequently felt cramped and resentful when there's been a man bidding for your time, *STOP* and think about what those feelings mean to you. Holding out on marriage requires tenacity and the ability to withstand social pressure from every corner—family, married friends, children, prospective mates. And these may not be the only pressures. You may also find yourself feeling guilty for not pleasing the "significant others" in your life and guilty for not being the kind of person who can march to the beat of a societal drum. Very likely you will experience a feeling that something must be "wrong" with you for choosing to be single. This would be true only if your decision was an imposition rather than a choice.

Deciding against marriage should be a conscious choice, one that involves a serious consideration of the consequences. Here are a few questions to help you: Will singledom look as good to me at 65 as it does at 35? (Of course, you can retract your decision along the way, but it may be more difficult later because there'll be fewer men and your lifestyle will have become more entrenched.) What do my female married friends say about marriage (the happily and unhappily married among them)? Will I be unfulfilled because I've missed out on this slice of life?

Don't add a Mrs. to your name *unless you want to*. To give this advice one last punch, I can tell you that in my therapy practice I've seen a few examples of marriage that were painfully dissolved because one of the parties blindly entered the marital state without really desiring it.

Myth #2: Marriage Solves the Problems of Aloneness and Loneliness.

If you don't remember anything else in this book, I hope you will remember this: *Marriage does not give you a lifetime warranty against aloneness or loneliness.*

Speaking first in the context of aloneness, let me say that marriage *is* a risk. Some day one of the mates is going to *lose* the other, and neither of you knows when that day will come. Each of you can predict that it will hurt when it happens and that one of you (or both) will be *alone*. If you never take the risk, then you don't have the pain of loss. Likewise, if you've never learned to enjoy your aloneness life can become chronically miserable after a divorce or a spouse's death. Getting married in order to prevent aloneness is like building a bomb shelter in anticipation of the holocaust. It's illusory protection.

Even without anything as wrenching as death or divorce, there are many periods of aloneness in marriage just as there are in single life. One of the conditions for sustaining a happy marriage is the ability to enjoy one's own good company.

Marriage, in and of itself, doesn't cure loneliness either, but *good* marriages do reduce its psychic toll. You can be as lonely in someone's presence as you can be when you're alone or in a roomful of strangers. Marital loneliness is especially painful, because it's so unexpected. When people get married, they assume that they will have an intimate connection with someone who understands and cares. After all, this is presumed to be the essence of love, and love is the typical rationale for entering into matrimony. The problem is that it is one thing to feel "in love" and quite another to have the skills to be loving. When, for one reason or another, each or both of the married partners are unable to communicate *lovingly*, loneliness is the inevitable outcome. Inasmuch as *love is a feeling* (a disputable definition, as will be seen in the last chapter), so *loving is a skill* demanding the lover's commitment, empathy, flexibility, and self-awareness. There is a potential pitfall here. One partner may unconsciously impose his or her standard for intimacy on the other. It's a good idea to remember that there are a lot of ways to show care, understanding, and connectedness. No *one way* is the right way. Nevertheless, it is true that people often fall in love, marry, and then neglect the activity of loving. If loving is ongoing in a marriage, then loneliness is sporadic and momentary.

Myth #3: My Marriage Partner Will Be the Embodiment of Everything I Lack, Or: What I Can't Be, He Will Be for Me.

Sally is shy, but she's always wished she were more outgoing, so she marries Sam. He's the life of the party. When they're out together with other people, he takes over. He brings her right into every conversation, forges their new friendships, and keeps interaction going whenever she falters. She thanks her lucky stars that she's got Sam by her side for every social occasion. She couldn't make it through without him.

Or let's take Carol's case. Carol is dissatisfied with her career, feels she's going nowhere, and can't seem to get out of the rut. Her husband, Chuck, is happy with his job, feels he's accomplishing things, and looks forward to going to work every day. Carol concludes that she and Chuck just aren't earning enough money to make ends meet. She decides to work on Chuck to persuade him that now's the time for him to think about moving up in his profession.

What do Sally and Carol have in common? Both of them are living *vicariously through* their marriage partners rather than *with* them. Sally has sidestepped her own problem with shyness by letting Sam do her socializing for her and Carol has displaced her career ambitions onto Chuck. Both Sally and Carol are functioning as half-people. It may work as long as Sam and Chuck remain oblivious to their complicity in these manipulative schemes, but both women are playing for high stakes at the marriage table. The chances are very good that Sam and Chuck will catch on to the fact that they're being used. Eventually, Sally and Carol will seem more like burdens than wives. Once both men feel their own identities slipping away, they'll be tempted to look for escape hatches.

Your marriage partner can't be the unfulfilled half of you. This doesn't mean that he should be your temperamental or personal carbon copy, or that he shouldn't be different from you (obviously it's impossible for him to be just like you), but it does mean that you can't expect *him* to make *you* complete.

To put it another way in conclusion, I'll paraphrase the title of a book by Gordon and Margaret Paul, *Do I Have to Give Up Me to Be Loved by You?** If I give up on all or part of me, how can he love the whole of me?

Myth #4: Marriage Doesn't Work—Look at All the Divorces.

It would be tempting to let the doomsayer win this one hands down. There's no question about it—the divorce rate is high. However, right alongside this gloomy news is the fact that remarriage rates are just as high and still climbing. Can any sense be made of these seemingly

---

* Gordon Paul, Ph.D., and Margaret Paul, Ph.D. *Do I Have to Give Up Me to Be Loved by You?* (Minneapolis, Minnesota: CompCare Publications, 1983).

incompatible pieces of information? After all, isn't it logical to assume that partners burned in previous marital frying pans would want to keep far away from fires? Human behavior is often illogical, and especially in regard to remarriage statistics. According to Simenauer and Carroll, most divorcees plan to go from the frying pan into the fire (if they haven't already done so). What this says to me is that *hope* can be at least as powerful as logic. When we don't do well the first time around, whether it's on tests for school or in our marriages, we frequently want to try again. Looked at from a historical perspective, there's the point that Merle Shain makes in her wonderful book, *Some Men Are More Perfect Than Others*: In bygone days people died at younger ages than they do now, so that, in some measure, death took the place of divorce in terminating marriages.* From whatever vantage point you want to look at it, marriage is the preferred lifestyle for most people, so if at first they don't succeed...! Divorce can be prevented *if* you put off marriage until you're ready for it and then choose your mate carefully. More will be said about this later. For now it suffices to remind you that marriages can and do work. However, once in a good marriage you need to be as creative and resourceful to sustain it as you had to be to find the man in the first place.

Now pause for a moment and consider whether or not you've had these myths in your suitcase. If you still want to go on our journey, you'll need to remove them. We have more unpacking to do. This time you have to deal with your own private doomsayer—that little voice that tells you that meeting Mr. Right is something that happens to other people but not to you. Next, I am going to recant what I think that voice may have been saying to you, and why I don't agree with it.

---

* Merle Shain, *Some Men Are More Perfect Than Others* (New York: Bantam Books, 1973), p. 89.

Myths About You

Myth #1: It's All a Matter of Luck and Chance— There's Nothing I Can Do to Meet Someone.

I'm starting off with this myth because it's the one that does the most damage. In my classes I hear it repeatedly, especially from women over 35. Females still cling tenaciously to the medieval definition of romance. According to this view, the knight on the horse rides up and sweeps her off her feet. The only significant alteration that has taken place in this fantasy which approximates present-day reality is that nowadays she waits for him to ride up in a nice car! Never mind that we live in an increasingly more anonymous, dangerous, and less intimate society, still she tells herself that for love to be real, he must spot her somewhere and then pursue her. Their eyes should meet and from then on it should be up to him. Unfortunately, there are several factors that she totally ignores. *First, she has to go someplace* for their eyes to meet. She can't be sitting alone in her apartment. *Second*, the chances are 50–50 at best that he will approach her. It's just as likely that she will notice him before he notices her. It's entirely possible, in fact, that she will never catch his eye unless *she does something* to attract his attention. Then, even if he does see her, there's no guarantee that he will pursue her. His failing to do so is not necessarily an indication of lack of interest.

So, ladies, let me reiterate—you're living in the 1980s, not the 1580s, and most of you are residing in large metropolitan areas with much-publicized crime rates and without benefit of cozy ties to families and neighbors! Many of you don't even go to church or temple every week anymore. By night, you're likely to be living in big apartment complexes where you're keeping steady company with a TV set. By day, you're competing in the cold and sometimes cruel world of the marketplace where you're advised not to mix intimacy with business. In such impersonal environments, love is unlikely to fall into your lap. *You're going to have to get out and find it by building your own networks and by taking advantage of whatever resources our society provides for you.* And once you're out there, *you're going to have to be prepared to do some of the pursuing and approaching yourself.*

Single men in my classes send out the same message over and over again: *They're tired and wary of making all the overtures and risking all the rejection.* There are many possible explanations for this stance, but the one that's most compelling for me comes from William Novak's interpretation of his conversations with single men as described in his book *The Great American Man Shortage.* He says, "Men feel as vulnerable as women in the conflict between the sexes. What women often fail to understand is that each side in the conflict sees itself as vulnerable and believes that the other side is very powerful."*

Myth #2: I'm too Old, too Unattractive, and/or too Rare a Bird to Find Anyone Who Will Like Me.

This is the familiar personal-faults myth or the "I don't have what it takes" syndrome. The damaging feature of this myth is that it gets an onslaught of validation from the media. I won't insult your intelligence by reiterating all the ways that the media (which is in cahoots with the clothing and cosmetic manufacturers) use to tell you that you are too old, too unattractive, or too odd, but I will take the risk of insulting you by saying that *I think you believe much more in what you see than in what you know.* In fact, the advertisers adore that quality in you! You *know* that if you're over 35 and alone, there are

* William Novak, *The Great American Man Shortage* (New York: Rawson Associates, 1983), p. 81.

other people out there like you. And not all the older men are looking for 21-year-olds. But you've seen just enough pictures of older men squiring glamorous, youthful women to *believe* that those men are representative of the whole damn pack.

Let's say you *know*, too, that you're not beautiful, and that there are lots of other people out there who aren't beautiful either—men and women. In fact, you know really homely women who've tied the knot. But every day, you're bombarded with visual images of beautiful women beaming into the eyes of admiring men, so you *believe* that these are the women who get the real men.

Finally, you *know* that you're unique. You don't dress like everybody else, wear your hair like them, or enjoy the same activities, and you *know* that if you're unique, there must be other unique men and women out there. You've even met some of them, but you don't see them as often as you see the smiling people on your TV screen or on the glossy magazine covers. You see those people as young, handsome look-and-do-alikes. You *believe* that you're so far removed from the mainstream that you must be living in the wrong country. Maybe you could find a man in Outer Mongolia who would have you, but certainly not in Manhattan!

So if you continue to believe what you see, at the expense of what you know, it's going to be tough to meet him.

Myth #3: There's Only One Person in the World Who's Right for Me, and the Odds for Meeting Him Are not in My Favor. If I haven't Already Met Him by Now the Chances Are I Never Will.

When you were a teen-ager and going steady, if your mother was anything like mine, she probably reminded you that there were "lots of fish in the sea." "No need to tie yourself down now," she'd say. Perhaps you took this motherly advice to heart and spent many years fishing.

As you got older, though, in your 20s and 30s, did you notice that mother stopped saying this? Whether it comes suddenly or gradually, you get the message that male fish are an endangered species. Apparently, the U.S. Census Bureau reached a similar conclusion. In 1983, they reported that there were 33,888,000 single women and 26,463,000 single men in the United States over the age of 18 (single includes never-married, divorced, and widowed people).* Clearly, these figures do add up to an American man shortage, and pessimistic statistical evidence does have a psychological impact. (One needs only to look at the effect of publicity about rising crime rates to understand this point. Women are more cautious and fearful on the streets and in their homes than they were even a decade ago.) It's a short leap, then, from learning that there are more single women than single men to the conviction that you will probably be one of those who's left out of the running. Taking the crime analogy a step further, however, no one would argue that it's prudent for women to take sensible precautions against criminal victimization, but does the same argument hold for finding a mate? Should women carry caution to the point of putting themselves out of the running? The answer to both questions is NO! This is a very big country and the world community is still bigger and more intertwined than ever before. That adds up to a whole lot of men and women! If you prefer, think about it from the perspective of looking for a job. We all know that almost every good job has numerous applicants bidding for it. We apply anyway and if we don't get one, we try for another. The same principle applies to finding a mate.

I'll arrive at the same optimistic destination by taking a different route as my last example, and my model will be the increasing numbers of educated black women in the United States, especially those over 30. For this pop-

* *Statistical Abstract of the United States 1985*, 105th edition, (U.S. Department of Commerce, Bureau of the Census), p. 48.

ulation of women, the black American man shortage is acute if men of similar educational standing are being sought. Not only are there fewer available men, but among them there are increasing numbers who marry interracially. It doesn't work equitably in the reverse, though, because even if a black woman might want to entertain the idea of marriage to a white man, racial prejudice operates more prevalently against her than against her male counterpart. (This is not to imply that it's nonexistent.) According to 1983 census figures, 118,000 black men were married to white women, whereas only 46,000 black women were married to white men.* As psychologist and writer Ann Poussaint, my good friend, says: "What this means to me is that these women must think about expanding their horizons beyond home turf in order to find mates." I'll have more to say about how they can do this in a later chapter, but for the moment it will suffice to say that for white women, as in other aspects of their daily lives (affirmative action notwithstanding), the man search is far easier by comparison. Because black women have always come by their achievements by working against the odds— through sheer courage, creativity, and determination— there is much that every woman can learn from their example. Are you going to lay down and die with a scarlet "Single" emblazoned on your breast or are you going to muster the energy and determination to stay the course?

In summary, if I were you—and I was until 15 years ago—I'd go with mother's advice rather than with Census Bureau statistics. (They were pessimistic then, too.) To me, it's not a matter of availability. The sea is still well stocked with male fish. It's more a matter of becoming a good angler, one who is as determined to succeed as she is clever with her equipment!

* *Statistical Abstract of the United States 1985*, p. 38.

Myth #4: There Aren't Any "Good" Men Left.

This is the place where the doomsayer in you really gets a grip. Maybe she's conceded that there are men out there, but she won't let go of the idea that the "good" men have all been taken. In Chapter 3, I'll share my thoughts about who the "good" men are, but for the moment let me assure you that they're not *all* taken. I meet some of them every week in my classes, and every time a new class begins I meet still more. (I teach a lot of classes.) I've made their acquaintance at parties, art galleries, and on airplanes as well.

Five years ago when I first started teaching these classes on mating I was inclined to believe the many women who told me emphatically that there weren't any "good" men left. After all, I hadn't been a part of the singles scene for 10 years. Maybe they were right—perhaps the quality of men had declined. But, after several years of listening to single women in the classes and in my private practice, I made a significant observation. Those women who parted company with their own negative attitudes and, at the same time, demonstrated an openness to experimentation with *new options* for meeting men were much more successful at finding "good" men than those who didn't. (More will follow about attitudes in Chapter 8.) This appeared to be true regardless of age, physical beauty, professional status, or prior experience with marriage. While I accept the statistical reality of the man shortage in general and the "good" man shortage in particular, I am just as convinced that the women who approach mating with positive and open-minded attitudes fare much better with men than those who heed the doomsayer. Negativity is like a bad cold—people want to keep their distance from the carrier!

Myth #5: Everyone Who Uses Dating Services and Other "Singles" Resources Is a Loser. If I Sign Up I'll be Marked as a Loser Too.

This notion is so prevalent that it could be classified as an epidemic that requires radical surgery for treatment! Not only does it not make sense for the times we live in, but it doesn't square with economic reality either. As I've said previously, *most of you no longer live in close-knit communities where Mom and Dad and the family next door have the time and interest to look for available men for you.* Instead, you are located in big cities or sprawling suburbs where it's tough to get a social foothold. Your neighbors, colleagues, and friends are too busy just earning a living and keeping their single or familial ships afloat. *Dating services and singles organizations have stepped in to fill a gaping void.* In case you haven't noticed, many of these organizations are thriving. When they fold, it's usually due to poor management, not a lack of demand for their services. You can be 100% sure that if our modern-day matchmaking entrepreneurs are showing a profit, they've got clients of both sexes. Since every American has been raised on the formula that "money talks," tell me how women can possibly believe that these services are catering exclusively to "losers" who nobody would ever want? Where's the profit in that?

Now I'm not saying that Mr. Right is guaranteed to be located at the other end of a computer terminal, but I am saying that for every "loser" who pops up (and remember that the term "loser" is purely subjective; a "loser" to me is not necessarily a "loser" to you), there's got to be at least a "non-loser" if not "the winner." From the annals of my students I could give you examples that run the gamut from no luck at all with dating services and singles organizations to instant success, i.e., the first date becomes the mate. More typical are stories in the middle: some good prospects, some lousy. Later on I'll say more about shopping for such services, but to sum up here, my husband has permitted me to steal a phrase he coined for our single friends when they complained about being out of romantic circulation. "What you need is a '*slump-breaker*,'" he advised them. Well, ladies, let me tell you—dating services are terrific "slump-breakers!"

. . . . .

At last we've unloaded the suitcase of its cumbersome contents. It's wiser to travel light, and, besides, you'll need space for the new items you'll be picking up en route.

We're not ready to pack yet. First, there's some advance work to be done on *you*.

CHAPTER 2

The Presenting of Me—Am I Who I Say I Am?

As your matrimonial tour director with a reputation to uphold, I am invested in making this a meaningful journey for you, so my next task is to involve you in an independent research project in preparation for a field trip.

Judging Books by Their Covers

"Don't judge a book by its cover," my mother would admonish me whenever I'd criticize someone for what she considered to be his or her superficial characteristics. I was too inexperienced then to contest her, but I know now that all of us are regularly engaged in the practice of judging books by their covers. If the cover looks enticing, we're much more likely to read the book. One can argue about the merits of relying on visual cues to accurately assess each other, but there is no denying that we do it.

Nowhere is this truth more obvious than in the mating game. Listen to some comments from single women in my classes:

"I went out with this guy, and I thought he was pretty nice until I saw him eating. It was disgusting. He didn't *chew* his food—he smacked it, making loud noises all the while. I didn't go out with him again."

Another student states, "I was at this singles' club and a man came over to me. He wasn't bad looking, but he had on a polyester leisure suit. I can't stand leisure suits. I decided to talk to someone else."

I doubt if there is any reader who can honestly say that she hasn't rejected a man for reasons as seemingly "foolish" as these. The fact is that you have done so and will continue to, whether or not you think it's fair. It's one of the little tricks that our eyes play with our minds, and our eyes usually win! So if we can agree that we judge men this way (and women too, for that matter), we can assume that men do likewise. Just to drive the point home, I'll tell you about an exercise I use in teaching. I ask the students, before they know each other well, to break into small groups and look at each person carefully. No talking—just looking. Then I instruct them to write down what they've observed about one another. After they've finished, I ask them to share their observations orally with the entire class. The wealth of information is amazing! Not only do they notice physical characteristics, but they surprise themselves with the number of psychological inferences they make. Here are two samples:

About Joan, who looked to be 40 plus, came to class nattily dressed, wearing jewelry and makeup, a female classmate said, "She's the kind of person who would like to get dressed up and go dancing. She'd always have something in her closet to wear. She seems like someone who thinks she's looking for a mate but she's really looking for a date."

A man in the class, speaking about a 30-ish female named Susie who sat in the back of the class and rarely spoke, "She's shy, but attractive. She doesn't present herself well though, so a man probably wouldn't know what she wants."

Because we unconsciously make many assumptions about people's internal selves from our observations of their external selves, this exercise raises our consciousness about how much we "read into" what we see. Joan's appearance may or may not indicate who she is looking for (a mate or a date), any more than Susie's apparent shyness can be linked conclusively with an inability to ask a man for what she wants. Still, it is valuable to Joan and Susie to know how they have been perceived by other people, especially if the same perceptions are repeated. For observer and observed alike, the *awareness* that this process of looking and assuming is a fixture of social relations offers *choices* that weren't there before. Now we can choose, when wearing our observer hats, *to test our assumptions verbally*: "Joan, are you a good-time girl who just likes to get dressed up and go out dancing with anyone, or are you interested in a lot of different activities with someone in particular?" Or, when being observed, to assert ourselves as if we were in Susie's shoes: "You may not have noticed, but I'm a little shy. Please don't take that to mean that I'm not interested in talking to you." Even the food-smacking and leisure-suited men can be approached gently and humorously at a propitious moment: "I've got to tell you right out front, Charlie, I've got this thing about eating habits, so if we're going to dine together I'd love it if you chewed quietly," and to the other man, "I don't know what it is about leisure suits that gets to me, but I think I'd better confess it to you. Is your whole closet full of them or just half of it?"

For the moment, we will focus on you—*the observed*—rather than you the observer. That part comes later.

The Outer You

Hopefully, you know by now that you're another female "book" who's being judged by her cover. You should know, too, that your cover has to look its best in order to attract potential male "readers." So the first thing you have to do is look in the mirror. The big question for the looking glass is, "Am I maximizing my attractiveness?" Here are some mini-questions to help answer the big one:

1. Do I highlight my best physical features with the right blend of cosmetics, clothing, and colors?
2. Do I have any physical features that are so detrimental to my appearance that I need to take action such as surgery, an intensive weight program, or dentistry, etc., to correct them?
3. What is my body language? Does my body look relaxed and contented, or is it slumped, taut, tense, or fidgety?
4. Do my hair, clothing, and general demeanor reflect the essence of me?

If you can't answer these questions affirmatively, or if you're unsure of the answers, get help from someone, i.e., a good cosmetician, a good friend, a good exercise teacher, a good apparel salesperson, or all four and more if need be. I stress the word *good* because many people are not *good enough* at what they do. In this context, *good* describes people who have an aesthetic sixth sense and know how to use it for the enhancement of you. The department store salesperson who sizes you up, and converts her visualization into an outfit that looks like you, is good at her job.

As someone who prides herself on being a good therapist, I confess that I pay increasing attention to question 4 when I see clients. So if I see a tall and slender single woman who has a sense of humor and a streak of the adventurer in her, I'll say, "I really don't think those vertically striped, slim-fitting pants and that tailored blouse are right for you." Then I gently prod her into considering clothes more flattering to her, something with fullness and flair, so that people can look at her horizontally as well as vertically. Likewise, with a petite, attractive, vivacious professional woman who dresses in tailored suits, I suggest she trade the jackets for sweaters or blouses that reveal a hint of skin around the neckline and a suggestion of a curvature in the region of the breasts, so that her outward appearance accurately reflects her personality.

Many women tell me how much they've appreciated this feedback from me, and I have no reason to doubt their word. We have become so inundated with media images telling us how we *should* look that we lose ourselves in the process of becoming fashionable. Thus, urban professional women today tend to resemble a suited army. For almost every identifiable group of women (and men), there is an attendant fashion image in our heads. This being so, the best advice I can give is to warn you against sacrificing your physical uniqueness to the fashion rank and file. Remember, to attract a man you need to stand out—ever so slightly—in the crowd. For some women, natural good looks and a shapely figure are enough, but for the physically imperfect majority of us, the application of creative touches can make all the difference.

The Inner You

Assuming that you've gotten the outer you in order, we can begin to take a look at the inner you. At the outset, however, I should emphasize that some of the inner you can be detected through the outer you without any demonstrable effort on your part to conceal or reveal. If you are a happy, self-confident person, it will show in your demeanor, regardless of clothing or cosmetics, just as it will be apparent if you are unhappy and lack confidence. Faces and bodies do speak without any help from the lips. They are especially adept at communicating happiness and unhappiness, self-esteem and low self-esteem, flexibility and rigidity. A smile from an unhappy person is a faint smile indeed. All of us have heard someone described as "sad looking." Conversely, content people project a look of happiness.

Before we can go much further, a personal stock taking is in order. Below are some questions to put to yourself first, and second, to people who care about you and know you well. The idea is to measure your assessment of yourself against others' impressions of you. If there are glaring differences between your outlook and theirs, or if you have nobody to put these questions to, you've got problems on your hands which I'll address later in this chapter.

QUESTIONNAIRE
1. Am I generally a happy, fulfilled person who derives joy from being myself?
   If *yes*, describe how.
   If *no*, why not? What have I done about it?
2. Rate those adjectives that describe you most accurately (use a scale from 1 to 5, with 1 being least accurate and 5 most accurate):

adventurous___   plain___   materialistic___

intellectual___   sexual___   dependent___

funny___   depressed___   responsible___

serious___   lonely___   disciplined___

intense___   cautious___   lazy___

unpredictable___ predictable___   energetic___

aggressive___   attractive___   smart___

sweet___   angry___   self-righteous___

shy___   outgoing___   indecisive___

self-sufficient___ athletic___   addictive___

passive___   helpless___   exciting___

talented___   indifferent___   nervous___

worried___   honest___   opportunistic___

self-centered___   talkative___   ambitious___

pretentious___   opinionated___   incapable___

sensitive___   compliant___   flighty___

flamboyant___   passionate___   *others
*Add others if you wish.   _____
                                         _____
                                         _____

3. What do I contribute to other people's lives?
4. What is most annoying about me?

5. What are the priorities in my life? Do I behave accordingly?
6. What are my skills and strengths? What are my ineptitudes and weaknesses?
7. What are my most cherished values, beliefs, and convictions?
8. Am I open or closed? How knowable am I?
9. Do I fall easily into ruts or repetitive self-defeating patterns?
10. Do I wear observable scars from childhood? If *yes*, what are they? (Example: See page 40.)

Once you have answered these questions about yourself, it will be up to you (with a little help from me) to evaluate your answers. Your own instincts represent the best judgment as long as you are honest with yourself. Don't try to make yourself look better or worse than you feel. Put stars by those answers that trouble you, and note the number of stars you have given yourself. If you see a page full of stars, don't panic! Self-discovery can be fun, even if there is a little pain in the process.

For the moment, put your own answers aside, and give the questionnaire to as many people who know and care about you as are willing and available to help you. Instead of asking them to evaluate and star each of their answers, put an 11th question to them: "If you were in my shoes, which of the topics on this questionnaire would you want me to work on in order for me to feel healthier and happier?"

You Have a Problem If . . .

To help you integrate this valuable data, I'm going to focus the discussion on potential problem areas, with full recognition of two unassailable facts: 1) *We all have problems* (nobody can come up with a star-free questionnaire), so it's a matter of their extent and degree, rather than their existence, that counts. 2) There is not a woman (or man) among us who couldn't, in the course of a lifetime, benefit from psychotherapeutic counseling. So if I appear to be perpetually tooting the therapeutic horn, it's not because I think we're all mentally ill, but rather because I know that occasionally it requires more motivation than we can muster by ourselves to keep on growing up. (For excellent reading on psychotherapy, I recommend *The Road Less Traveled*, by M. Scott Peck, M.D., Touchstone Books.)

Before I take up each question separately, there are a few general statements to be made. As I mentioned earlier, *you have a problem worthy of attention if there are obvious discrepancies between your perception of yourself and other people's perception of you.* Assuming you have enlisted people who know you and generally care for you, it is then safe to say that either you are not presenting yourself as the person you believe yourself to be, or you are not the person you think you are. Whichever is the case, you need to make a correction. (This is one instance where the services of a therapist can be extremely useful.) Any potential Mr. Right will want to know the real you. *You have a problem worthy of attention if you have no one you can ask to work on your questionnaire.* This has to mean that you are isolated and do not allow people to know you. Without the experience of solid friendships under your belt, it's going to be hard for you to share yourself with a man or vice versa. While some sessions with a therapist would be beneficial to you, it is equally important for you to get out into the world, posthaste, and begin interacting with your peers. Finally, *you have a problem worthy of attention if you have no starred items on your questionnaire.* It's impossible to go through life problem-free, without edges that need reshaping, so you need someone to shake you out of your complacency. It might as well be me!

Now let's take a look at each question with an eye toward identifying "red flags."

Question 1: If you've answered "no" to this question, it's important for you to try to get at the source of your unhappiness, and to do whatever you can to make your life more rewarding. This may mean making changes in your circumstances such as job, living arrangements, geographic location, friendship network, or family entanglements. Although changes like these can seem scary initially, they are often the right medicines for a malaise, especially if it feels like a rut. If you can't find the source of your discontent, a good therapist may be able to help you solve the mystery. The important message to heed here is that you owe it to yourself to do something about your unhappiness. It won't just disappear of its own accord.

Question 2: There are a lot of adjectives on this list which are open to subjective interpretation. For example, someone might describe herself as "intense," and regard that as a positive characteristic, while someone else might see it as a negative trait. If you assign negative connotations to many of the adjectives that you think are descriptive of you, first try to determine whether or not you can find a positive connotation for the word. Example: *Seriousness* can be as much a positive quality as a negative one, but if you regard it as a negative, then perhaps it's your *attitude* that needs changing. Maybe your mother always said, "You're too serious, why don't you lighten up?" and you assumed that she was right. Go down your list of negative adjectives and see how many you can convert to positives. Then focus on the remaining ones (there should be a few) that you can't budge from the negative column. What are you going to do about them? Let me give you some simple, workable advice: *Change them.* (I'm not asking you to change your whole personality, I'm just suggesting that you wash a little dirty linen!)

Question 3: This is my favorite question, especially in this era when it's easy to get the notion that all we have to do is turn our attention to ourselves. Popular wisdom would have us believe that we need only look good, feel good, know ourselves, exercise, and make money. If only that were true—but unfortunately it's a boldfaced lie. You can do all of that and still wind up on the losing end of the mating game. The best women (and men) are those who understand that the way to the human heart is through the personal gifts that we bestow: the *sharing* of our talents, the *lift* our presence gives to someone, the *contributions* we make to families, friends, colleagues, society. In one of my Spouse Hunting classes, I asked people what they did best. A middle-aged woman replied that she was a fabulous cook. I asked her if she shared this talent with other people. Sadly, her answer was "no." Of course she was having difficulty finding Mr. Right. She hadn't been willing to share the best of herself! Do you get the point? If you can't think of any contributions that you make to other people, you're in trouble. Go right out and offer your services somewhere.

Question 4: We all have our quirks, but some are more annoying than others. What you're looking for here are characteristics that *repeatedly* get in your way—things that turn people off often enough to warrant remediation. Examples: The kind of person who never lets anyone finish talking without interrupting. The kind of person who talks nonstop about herself without ever asking a question about her companion(s). In contrast, the kind of person who sits back and expects the other person to do all the talking. This question is especially useful when put to your friends. Because we frequently are *unaware* of our most unappealing and habitual traits, the *conscious awareness* of these can be enough to jolt us into corrective action. If you can't break a debilitating habit, you might want to get some help from a therapist.

Question 5: It's easier to talk about our priorities in life than it is to act on them. Without a doubt, readers of this book would proclaim unanimously that finding a husband is a high, if not the #1, priority. I've heard it stated on countless occasions in my classes, but invariably, I find a huge gap between the desire and the implementation. *Wanting* a good husband is not the same as *actively seeking* one, and the same can be said for many of our dreams. The sad part of this is that so many of us never learn that our *recurrent dreams should be our priorities*. Instead, we discount dreams as mere fantasies so that they can never become priorities. I suspect that there are thousands of women who can't prioritize, because they can't listen to their dreams. It's true that some dreams are beyond our grasp, but for every one that is, there's one that isn't. When I was much younger, I dreamt of becoming a torch singer or an author. Over time, the first dream faded. I didn't have the goods. The second one persisted, and here I am. There was another dream in between—to be married to a good husband. I went after that one, too. It worked. If you're *not doing something* to realize your dreams, you've got a problem. *Take some action*—almost anything you do is better than nothing. It's not *what you want*, but *what you do about what you want* that makes all the difference.

Question 6: You've had to answer this question thousands of times for application blanks and interviews, so it should be easy. I'm asking it to make sure that *you know* your strengths and weaknesses and that *other people know them, too*. Hopefully, you can acknowledge your strengths and let other people enjoy them. Don't keep them to yourself. Once you've recognized your strengths, it's a good idea to be acquainted with your weaknesses, too. You can accept your less competent side more easily when you know your strengths. Obviously, if you find more incompetencies than competencies, you've got a problem: You don't think much of yourself. A good therapist can help you work on self-esteem. Mr. Right can't make you like yourself. You have to like you in order for him to like you.

Question 7: There is no more fundamental question in the mating game than this one, but it is frequently overlooked. It goes to the heart of compatibility. I will use myself as an example to clarify the point. Initially, it startles the students in my classes when I announce that I wouldn't have married a staunch political conservative. Only after I explain that my politics are too entrenched and too important to me to live with someone who doesn't share them, does the message hit home. If you search your soul, you should find there a set of beliefs, values, and convictions that you cherish. These are to be distinguished from interests and hobbies which, in my opinion, don't require the same mutuality. Although it's nice to have common interests in a partnership, diversity can be just as enriching. Here I am speaking of the principles that guide our lives, be they social, religious, moral, political, psychological, humanitarian, scientific, ethical, or a combination of many. These principles define your personhood as much as your personality does. You have a problem if you can't identify any, and you have a problem if you would sacrifice them for the temptation of expedient love. There is no better prescription for incompatibility in marriage than joining hands with someone who doesn't share deep-rooted values with you. Nor is marriage enhanced when one or both partners lack values altogether. So, if you couldn't come up with any answers to this question, it's very likely that your friends won't have been able to either. You need to reclaim your soul. Therapy or some form of spiritual counseling may be in order for you.

Question 8: This question has special meaning for people who tend toward shyness, pretentiousness, or rigidity. We all need people in our lives who know and understand us, but in order to receive those rewards, we must open ourselves to being known. If you hide, pretend, or shut down, you aren't knowable. When you're not knowable, you're lonely. You may see yourself as rejected, but in fact you are rejecting. Many shy people are surprised to learn that their withdrawn behavior can easily be interpreted as rejecting. Nowadays, adult-education classes on self-improvement abound. In short-term courses, one can acquire skills in assertiveness, body awareness, communication, and in how to approach the opposite sex. If such programs are available in your area, I recommend them as comparatively inexpensive and efficient ways to learn to be more knowable. In Chapter 6, I will say more about what you can do if your community lacks these and other resources.

Question 9: This question is begging for women who suffer from what I like to call the "automatic pilot syndrome." They never take a risk. They do things the way they've always done them and probably the way their mothers did them. They're convinced that things can't be done any other way. Of course, they're bored and long for someone to set off firecrackers underfoot because they don't have the slightest idea how to ignite their own. They're routine-addicted.

If you're on automatic pilot, make a solemn vow to yourself that you'll do one new thing every day and one old thing in a different way every day. Make sure that you enjoy the new activities that you've selected. The idea is to get yourself off course. Remember mother's old adage, "Things happen when you least expect them." I'd add to that, "and when you're not on automatic pilot."

Question 10:   What you're looking for here are the remnants of those old psychological bruises from childhood. As an example, let's assume your parents were the kind who never kept their promises to you. You're 32 now and it's hard for you to trust anybody, so you're cautious with your confidences. You don't tell anybody anything about you. "It's none of their business," you tell yourself confidently. It hasn't dawned on you that just because Mom and Dad were untrustworthy, it doesn't mean that everyone is like them. Some people may be, but certainly not everybody. Could it be that you haven't risked giving anyone a chance? We outgrow some of these childhood scars, but others linger. Try to identify those of yours that are still visible to you and your friends. Reassess them in the light of your present-day reality. Maybe you can confide in Peggy after all; maybe you don't have to argue with your boss just because he or she is an authority figure like your Mom or Dad; or maybe you don't have to go around trying to please everybody all the time in order to be accepted, even if your parents made you feel that that was the condition for *their* love. (There will be more discussion of childhood scars in Chapter 7.) If this doesn't work, try David Viscott's self-analysis instructions as outlined in Chapter 4 of his book *The Viscott Method—A Revolutionary Program for Self-Analysis and Understanding.**

Now What?

O.K., you've got all this information about yourself— what do you do with it? If I were you, I'd treat it like you did when you had to write a paper for school. You organize your data. You might want to divide the infor-

---

* David Viscott, M.D., *The Viscott Method*, (Houghton Mifflin Co., Boston 1984).

mation into three lists: List I—Positive Things About Myself That I Want to Highlight. List II—Problem Areas That I Want to Work On. List III—Plans for Attacking the Problem Areas. This last list is the most crucial. By now you should know that I believe in taking constructive action to solve problems. I've mentioned some suggestions already in this chapter, but I haven't begun to cover all the possibilities. You will need to devise plans that can be tailored to your financial resources, your time constraints, and your knowledge of those strategies for change that would offer the best prognosis for you.

A Word About Therapy

Because I have suggested psychotherapy so often as a way to deal with personal problems, I think it warrants further discussion.

Twenty-five years ago, psychotherapy was widely regarded by the public as a form of treatment for the mentally ill among us or for a selected few (usually affluent) mentally healthy people who suffered from comparatively minor psychological complaints. In this latter group belonged many mental health professionals for whom personal psychotherapy was an adjunct to their training. Also in this group were lay people who had the financial resources and the time to commit to what was typically a prolonged process of self-discovery leading to a hoped-for recovery.

Nowadays, the picture has changed dramatically. Most employees have insurance coverage for mental health services included in their fringe-benefit packages, with the result that they are now accessible to a broad socio-economic cross-section of the population. Furthermore, many states subsidize mental health services through Medicaid, so that low-income people are eligible to receive them. Not only has there been a huge increase in the numbers of people utilizing psychotherapeutic services, but there has also been a concomitant rise in the number of therapeutic modalities on the market. New forms of psychotherapy sprout up like wildflowers all over the country to compete for their share of the big mental health pie. To complicate matters, there are almost as many varieties of therapists as there are modalities. Hence, there are psychiatrists, psychologists, social workers, psychiatric nurses, counselors, lay therapists, healers, and family, marriage, and divorce specialists, among whom there are wide variations in quality of service, fees, and methods of practice. The choices are staggering, especially in large urban areas. Most states have a listing of licensed practitioners who are eligible to receive insurance payments.

Having acquainted you, in a very general way, with the intricate lay of the therapeutic landscape, I want to assure you that there are ways to work your way through the maze. *First*, let me state emphatically that going to see a therapist does not mark you as an oddball. *Everybody's doing it so don't think you're alone.* Even the therapists themselves are doing it!

So, you go shopping. You ask friends who they'd recommend. Word of mouth is often the best way to find someone. (Seventy-five percent of my clients are referred to me by other clients.) Or you ask your physician, minister, or rabbi. Get two or three names. It's a good idea to find out as much as you can about a prospective therapist over the telephone before you go in and meet him or her. You want to know: 1) What is the fee? 2) How many visits will your insurance cover? 3) How does he or she work, i.e., long-term or short-term, individual or group? Does he or she have experience with single people (some therapists work exclusively with couples, families, and/or children). 4) What are his or her qualifications? My personal bias is that experience, empathy, and intuitive intelligence are more important than credentials.

Often you can tell from the phone conversation whether the person seems right for you.

If you decide to go for one visit, you're not obligated to return. Therapy is much more effective *if you and the therapist like each other.* In this sense, selecting a therapist is somewhat akin to selecting a mate, except that you don't have to live together. It's O.K. to look around until you find the right one.

In closing, there is one other point that I want to make. Think of therapy as if it were vocational training. You invest a sizeable sum of money, you work hard, and your reward comes in the form of a desirable job. When single women come to me saying that they want to learn how to find and keep a lasting and satisfying relationship with a man, I take them at their word. (Occasionally we discover that a woman has been deceiving herself in this desire.) The therapy is aimed at that goal, and the client does whatever has to be done to get there. This may mean digging up the past and discovering and discarding worn-out psychological artifacts, it may be simply a matter of reshuffling present-day behaviors and attitudes, or it may be a combination of both. However the problem is defined, the solution is *action-oriented.* Thus, my single people's "college of therapy" costs money (although I do occasionally grant financial aid in the form of lowered fees), and requires weekly fieldwork assignments as prerequisites for graduation into matrimony. I like to see people get what they want!

. . . . .

In your big suitcase go these items that you have selected to portray the outer you to maximum advantage.

Now, you can gather up the personal data you've collected and put it neatly in your carry-on luggage. You will need to refer to it frequently as you travel.

CHAPTER 3

If I'm O.K., Who's O.K. for Me?

My father was a traveler. From his years of globetrotting, he passed on to me the idea that traveling and seeing were inextricable. Later, in my own travels, I learned that good eyesight didn't guarantee good observation since occasionally I overlooked splendors that had been in my path of vision, or I gazed too long at sights unworthy of attention. That can also happen when you're looking for a man.

It's time for takeoff, but don't bring cameras, just good eyes (and glasses—if you need them). Now you have a turn to be the observer. Before your journey ends, you will have perfected this skill.

The Mr. Wrongs—Sights Better Left Unseen

There are some men who aren't worthy of any woman's attention if she is serious about finding a mate. I wish that I didn't have to say this, but experience has taught me that many women lose their thinking caps when they get involved with men. These are the women who ride into relationships on clouds of "chemistry" only to discover, sometimes too late, that clouds are unreliable transport vehicles and chemicals can explode! Below are some categories of men whose "chemistry" is lethal when compounded with yours (in all of these categories there are men who have recovered from debilitating habits and behaviors, thus they are not included on the following "blacklist"):

1. *Substance-abusers:* Alcohol- and drug-addicted men are nothing but trouble. Never, never, never assume that you can save him from his addictions once he's hooked on you. You can't. The chance that he might clean up his act is so slight that it's not worth the risk. Even if he did eventually succeed, you would have paid so dearly for it yourself that by the time his recovery occurred, yours would be a long way off.

2. *Gamblers and corrupters:* Any man who can't keep himself away from the betting booths or who engages in corrupt practices is a poor risk for marriage. His unethical behavior is seldom confined to smoke-filled parlors outside the home and its repercussions spread. The behavior and the man are a package deal. When you marry him, you marry his behavior as well.

3. *The mentally ill:* Unfortunately, there are some men who suffer from *debilitating* mental illness such as

psychosis, chronic depression, psychopathic behavior, or serious character problems. They make poor mates because a healthy dose of emotional stability is a necessary ingredient for each partner in a workable marriage. This is not to suggest that you avoid men who experience intermittent psychological distress, or those who have it under control through therapy and/or medication. As I said in the preceding chapter, it's impossible for anybody to go through life totally free of psychological stress and strain.

4. *The unavailable:* This category is harder to pinpoint than the above three, but just as important. The most obvious subgroup consists of *married men. Men with wives are not available as mates.* Already I can hear the choral refrain, "What about the men who eventually divorce their wives in order to marry their lovers?" I'll concede that it does happen, but that's as far as I'll bend. For every man that does, there are ten who don't, and I'm very suspicious of the *one* who does. Everyone needs a little healing and personal-inventory time after a marriage ends. When one woman replaces another without a break in between, she's got the same odds against her that the first wife had. Since the majority of married men don't leave their wives for the "other woman," there is no point wasting your time in anticipation.

The next category of unavailable men are the kind I like to call the *elusive ones.* If they're unmarried, they're hard to identify. In fact, you need 20–20 vision to spot them. Oh, they are charming. As Drs. Connell Cowan and Melvyn Kinder describe them in *Smart Women, Foolish Choices,** they are the more endearing for their extensive knowledge of women. They are hearts and flowers

---

* Dr. Connell Cowan and Dr. Melvyn Kinder, *Smart Women, Foolish Choices* (New York: Clarkson N. Potter, 1985), p. 76.

and tenderness one minute, and out of sight the next! Even their excuses have flair. They're so busy doing important things that they can make you feel special for being intermittently included. They are the supreme performers of romantic tragedy. What makes them more irresistible is that they are apt to be financially successful and sensually appealing. They slip into and slide out of countless relationships, and even if they marry, they're not really available to their wives. They are the "me" men and there are lots more of them out there nowadays than there were a few generations ago. As author William Novak explains, our society has lately spawned more men who've never had to struggle in the fields of poverty or war, but instead have arrived at successful destinations through the doors of comfort and affluence. Accustomed as they are to instant gratification, attention, and favor, they *expect* it rather than *earn* it, and the dosages they receive are rarely sufficient for their appetites.* They're dependent men who require constant care. When women need something from them, they head for the exits. Psychologists call this breed of human beings narcissists, and although some are women, more of them are men.

Another classification of unavailable men are the *triangulators*. Although married men fall into this group, I'm speaking here about unmarried men. These men play one woman against another, or one woman against mother, job, or ex-wife. You never know where you stand with them, and they don't want you to know. The triangle is put in place to keep them at a safe distance from you and whoever else is located at the third point.

The final category of unavailable men are the *commitmentphobic* types as described by Maxine Schnall in *Limits: A Search for New Values.* To some extent, this is a catchall category, because womanizing married men;

---

* William Novak, *The Great American Man Shortage* (New York: Rawson Associates, 1983), p. 57.

elusive, narcissistic men; and triangulators can be classified as suffering from many, if not all, of the symptoms of commitmentphobia. Still, there are men whose behavior doesn't place them neatly into any of the above three categories, but who can be fairly labeled as commitmentphobic. As Schnall points out, the distinctive characteristic of the commitmentphobic male is his propensity *to equate commitment with entrapment or engulfment*. His fear of intimacy may drive him in the direction of random promiscuity, lonely isolation, or a perpetual search for "more" and "better" in his relationships with women.*

. . . . .

The 1960s and 1970s, let us not forget, was the era that gave birth to the new sexual freedom, and the women's liberation movement. It was also the time when the flower children were disowning parental models, one of which was the model of all those moms and dads locked into lifelong, emotionally bankrupt marriages. Many men concluded that it was better to love everybody, have sex with anybody, and seek self-fulfillment than to be ensnared in a committed relationship. The newly liberated women were a different breed than their mothers had been, and though they still desired love and commitment, they wanted independence, sexual freedom, and parity in the marketplace and on the home front. They expected a lot more from a mate than their mothers would have in their wildest dreams. Like their male counterparts, they were looking for "more" and "better" in the spheres of both work and love.

Thus, today's woman, particularly if she's middle or upper class and well educated, bears no resemblance to the submissive, obedient housewife of yesterday. Although she is by no means the cause of male commit-

---

* Maxine Schnall, *Limits: A Search for New Values* (New York: Clarkson N. Potter, 1981), p. 156.

mentphobia, she represents a significant threat to the commitmentphobic man who feels he has more to lose with her. He can't control her. Maybe she'll want more from him than he can give. If he gets hooked on her, she may abandon him. (Nowadays she doesn't even have to have him for financial support.) To make matters worse, he fears he can't please her sexually unless he performs better than her previous lovers, so he intensifies his commitmentphobia with performance anxiety.*

The fallout from all these new freedoms is everywhere in evidence. Male commitmentphobia is one example. On the female side of the slate, there seems to me to be a similar, disturbing trend. The most jarring discovery that I've made in my work with single women is that many of them have succumbed to the "more" and "better" principle in their search for "committed" mates. Often, they behave as their own worst enemies by assuming that the *trappings* of success in the marketplace are the indicators of success in love.

Mr. Rights—The Sights to See

When you've been sightseeing, perhaps it wasn't always the beautiful monuments that captured your imagination. Maybe it was some unheralded scene you happened upon, off the beaten tourist path, that took your breath away. So it often is with men. *The best men are not necessarily the best-looking men.* It is precisely because we have become so accustomed to judging books by their covers that I reiterate this point. In fact, I wish I had a nickel for every single woman in my classes who has spurned a man on looks alone. On this husband-hunting trip, we're going to look for nice people of the male spe-

* *Ibid.*

cies and if they're good-looking, so much the better. So who are these "good" men? (I'll discuss where you might find them in Chapter 5.) The good men are:

1. *Men who like women as people.* I met an experienced ladies' man once who professed to like women more than men. He was married, but with women who attracted him he was seductive and flirtatious. Never with his wife. If women suggested to him that his behavior was provocative, he disavowed responsibility for it. They were reading too much into it, he'd say. With his wife, he was publicly cantankerous or otherwise nonattentive. Through him I learned that men who make proclamations about their fondness for women are rarely very fond of them. *Men who genuinely like women are men who don't need to control women to satisfy egotistical needs. Men who are happy with themselves are the ones who enjoy women being women.* It can't be any other way. There is a suspicion that underlies women's fears about men who have few, if any, male friends. The question behind the fear is: If they don't share themselves with other men, the way women do with their female friends, how can they like themselves? Sometimes it's hard to tell whether a man's distance from male friendship is the result of self-deprecation or societal constraints. It's just as likely to be the latter.

    When I was single in the '60s, women my age (in their late 20s) were apt to be competitive with one another over men. In the last 20 years, I have noticed that women have made great progress in their relationships with one another. Increasing intimacy between women has ushered in on its coattails a spirit of cooperation rather than competition vis-à-vis men. I have been impressed by the frequency with which the women in my classes offer to help each other meet men.

Men, on the other hand, do not seem to be as
eager for supportive male friendships or social networks. Due to the fact that it's still a man's world,
to some extent, men can afford complacency. There
are more available women for them to choose from
than vice versa, and they've been groomed to be
self-reliant in the world of work as well. Add to
this the prevailing mood of homophobia among
heterosexual men, and it becomes easier to understand why men keep safe distances between themselves. All this notwithstanding, during my last
year or so of teaching, I have observed a heartening
transformation on the male front. Where once my
classes were attended exclusively by women, now
they are apt to be evenly distributed between the
sexes. In some instances, men have been in the
majority! With a little encouragement from me (for
which I can be counted upon), male students have
responded enthusiastically to my standard request
that the class structure itself into an ongoing support network to assist one another in the mating
process. (There will be more about networking in
Chapter 6.)

2. *Men who are honest.* If I had to name one character
trait that is the most important for human beings
to possess, I'd choose honesty. Dishonesty can, and
usually does, behave like cancer. It originates in
one area of a person's human-relations network
and gradually invades all the other areas. Both
sexes are afflicted by it, but historically men have
acquired the worst reputations for it.

With all due respect to the vast numbers of honest males, I believe that far too many of these un-
favorable reputations have been deserved!

At this point in our travels, let's stop and make a collective vow to look exclusively for honest men. I'll tell
you how to spot them. They *don't* engage in shady prac-

tices at work or elsewhere. They're *respected* and *liked* by colleagues and friends. They deliver on their promises; their words match their deeds. They don't substitute exploitation for admiration. They take responsibility for their behavior, and the behavior itself is never characterized by deviousness.

3. *Men who enjoy intimacy.* This is so obvious that it shouldn't require much elaboration. Most men would claim that they *desire* intimacy with a woman, but fewer men have the ability to *revel* in it when it's there. Instead, they circumvent its pleasure with a variety of disguises. They substitute sex for intimacy, dependency for intimacy, possessiveness for intimacy, work or extracurricular and extramarital activity for intimacy, time constraints for intimacy, the newspaper or television for intimacy. The list of substitutions is endless. They avoid it as if it were an addiction with a health warning. Some men, though, enjoy it immensely, and don't think it's dangerous. Do you know who they are? They're men who like being known by a woman and knowing her. They encourage her growth and their own growth even if it means increasing independence in a relationship. They communicate openly and listen attentively. They're affectionate.

4. *Men who enjoy life.* A wise man I know told me once that most people live out their lives just waiting to die. I took his statement to mean that these people function on a business-as-usual axis from early adulthood to death. I've thought a lot about his idea ever since I heard it, because it struck me that it's often hard to detect whether one is functioning on the death track or the life track, and harder still to change course if you're on the wrong route. Nonetheless, it's infinitely more rewarding to be married to a life-track man (assuming of

course that you can attract him because you are so alive). How can you identify men who are glad to be alive? Here's how I do it (and I do it about women, too). These are men who get turned on by possibilities, ideas, and experiences. They can be *explorers*—eager to venture into the unknown—or they can be *craftsmen*—building on what they know. They can put the routines and responsibilities of daily living into proper perspective. *Rather than be mastered by routine, they master it.* They do what they have to, all the while enjoying what is required and what is chosen. They put as much energy into what doesn't have to be done as into what does. They're forever seeking things that aren't required.

Not long ago on a trip to the Dominican Republic, my husband and I met an artist from whom we bought a painting. Several years before, he had been exiled from his country for his efforts on behalf of sugar-cane workers. During that time, he had lived in Europe. Finally, he was permitted to return home. He had 11 children and a partially blind wife. He earned a meager living from the sale of his paintings and lived in a two-room barrio. Still, he insisted that we share a meal with him and his family. He used the money we spent on his painting to buy the groceries. It was the happiest meal I've ever had, and he was the most alive man either of us had ever known. His curiosity had no limits. We could see that his spirit had infected his children and his wife, inspiring them to experience great joy, even in the face of hardship.

5. *Men who can give and receive without strings attached.* These are glorious men. They can share their feelings with you openly, whether positive or negative, and can be attentive to yours. They value your output and their own input and this generosity of spirit pervades their behavior. They *share*:

feelings, ideas, problems, money, possessions, gifts, caretaking, responsibilities, time, and talents, and they *appreciate and welcome your in-kind donations.* They do not keep mental scorecards, tallying up your debts against their gifts or vice versa. Instead of *assuming* that you should know their needs and how to meet them, they *tell you* what they need and how you can help. And if, occasionally, you can't deliver, they don't add your indisposition to a list of outstanding debts.

6. *Men who laugh and men who cry.* Funny people are good company, and if a man's not funny himself, then he at least needs to know how to laugh when you or someone else is funny. He doesn't have to *be* Woody Allen to see some of the absurdity that's all around us. Men without a sense of humor are psychologically impaired and very poor company. They don't wear well, and they hold up even worse under life's inevitable stresses. Without humor, fun is hard to come by, and life without fun is no life at all. Beware of men who never laugh, and beware of men who never cry, although here you need more leniency. Maybe it's too much for women to expect to meet men who can actually shed a tear or two. It's possible that the taboos against it are still too ingrained. But I have reason, from my experience as a therapist, to believe that this is another place where men have progressed. Inasmuch as absurdity is everywhere, so too is tragedy and pain. It's inconceivable to me that any man could march through life without sorrow coming close enough to spill over into tears. To be sure, there are ways to express it indirectly (among the most common are blame, withdrawal, or diffuse anger), but they are inadequate to the task and very prone to finding undeserving victims. Men who meet sadness head-on are better men, but many still have to learn how to do it when they are well into adulthood.

Women are always talking about how much better they feel after a good cry. Why should it be any different for men? The very act of crying is in itself a cleansing process. It is one of nature's ways of releasing pain.

7. *Men who are aware of the world around them.* In today's fast-paced, technological society, it's not surprising that people feel out-of-touch with each other and with the world. Maybe if the human brain came equipped with a fast-forward button, we could keep up with ourselves, but alas it does not, so making sense out of everything that's happening around us has become increasingly difficult. It's even more tempting to curl up in a cocoon spun from yesterday's values instead of today's realities. Good men, though, don't succumb to this temptation. They do as much as they can to stay abreast.

For our purposes here, let's look at the relationship between the sexes. What do good men need to know? They recognize that *women have changed* in the last 20 years. Modern women expect more from life, from men and from the world outside home than they once did. These good men understand, too, that both sexes (especially in the more affluent Western democracies) have abundant freedom nowadays. We have a staggering array of choices about everything from the consumer items we can buy to the ways we want to behave. Take sex as an example. Most of the old sexual taboos have gone by the boards. Now, masturbation is O.K., sex (and very likely a lot of it) before marriage is O.K., sex with someone other than your mate after marriage is commonplace, if not quite O.K., and homosexuality is making an inroad into being O.K. Men and women simply don't play by the same old rules anymore. Woe be it to the man who insists that his modern-day loved one conduct herself the way his mother or grandmother did.

It is no wonder that we so often speak of intimate relationships in the context of "work." Good men do continuously *work* on reshaping their social attitudes and values to bring them in line with the world as it is.

As I'm writing this, I'm thinking of a family I saw in my office recently. The father was a handsome man in his late 50s whose parents had instilled in him the necessity of hard work in order to provide all the good things of life for his wife and children. Trouble was that he had long since acquired more good things than they needed, but he was never around to enjoy his wife, his children, or those good things because he was breaking his back to accumulate more good things! It had never occurred to him that they would be happy just to have *him*, and that he had already succeeded at what he had set out to accomplish. He had been unable to subject his worn-out value to the test of present-day reality. The whole family was suffering from his compulsive behavior.

8. *Men who like themselves (self-esteem).* I saved the most important criterion for last. *If a man doesn't like himself, he's not going to be good at liking you.* Nobody will disagree with me on this point, but someone very well might ask, "How can you tell when a man genuinely likes himself?" The question itself presumes that there's potential for a "cover-up." Self-esteem can be feigned, but not for long, that is, if you know how to identify the real stuff.

Before proceeding to define and identify self-esteem, let me pass on a word of caution. It's rare to meet a 100% self-esteemed individual, because for most of us self-esteem is cumulative—an *evolving process* rather than an *inherited character trait* (like a snowball that gathers more size as it rolls along until it becomes big enough to be a snow-man). All of us, though, have the potential to come close to the mark.

Psychologist and author Nathaniel Branden, in his book *Honoring the Self*, defines the person with high self-esteem as someone who possesses a *combination* of *self-confidence*—a person who feels competent to know, to choose, to meet life's challenges, and to map the course his or her life will take—and *self-respect*—someone who feels worthy of happiness, caring, love, and respect.* If this description fits for people who have self-esteem, what describes people with "make-believe" self-esteem? Branden says they derive their sense of worthiness not from their own consciousness or from rationality, honesty, responsibility, and integrity, but rather from more easily attainable sources such as a sense of duty, or obligation, stoicism, or altruism, financial success, sexual attractiveness, or toughness.† Typical examples of pseudo-self-esteem are to be found in persons whose adult lives are guided by other people's or society's "shoulds and shouldn'ts," i.e., the man who has to make a lot of money to prove to his parents that he is a success, or the woman who gives her all to administer to other people without regard for her own needs, integrity, or personal growth. By a more apparent measure, "pretend" self-esteem comes in the form of arrogance, bragging, or the competitive drive to establish one's own superiority. All of the above examples revolve around controlling the fear of taking responsibility for being one's own person or delighting in one's own selfhood.

So, if the above *defines* self-esteem, what iden-

* Nathaniel Branden, *Honoring the Self* (Los Angeles: Jeremy Torcher Inc., 1983), p. 12.

† *Ibid.*, p. 15

tifies people who have it? Here I am again indebted to Nathaniel Branden, who took a sampling of opinion from a wide range of mental health clinicians. In summarized form, I'll reiterate the clues that his survey provides, and add a few of my own. I'll list these in the third person masculine, since it's self-esteeming men we're looking for:

- His affect, manner, and movement reflect joy in being alive and have a relaxed and spontaneous quality.
- He is open, direct, and honest about personal strengths and weaknesses, failures and successes.
- He can give and receive compliments and accept criticism comfortably.
- His words are compatible with his behavior.
- He is open to and curious about new or unfamiliar knowledge and experience.
- He is humorous, flexible, loving, creative, playful, assertive, and sad (when need be).
- Under stress, he maintains dignity and composure.
- He values his own and other people's time.
- He is empathic—he can put himself into others' shoes.
- His body signals are: alert, lively eyes; relaxed and natural facial postures; relaxed and erect shoulders; graceful, quiet hands; and relaxed arms.*

Up to this point, we've confined ourselves to learning how to sightsee in order to get maximum information from our eyes. Now we're moving into a new phase. Let's call it *cultural acclimation*. Next, I'm going to prepare you to interact with some good men. Don't worry if it all seems "foreign" to you at first.

* *Ibid.*, pp. 16 & 17.

CHAPTER 4

How to Get Mentally Ready to Meet Mr. Right

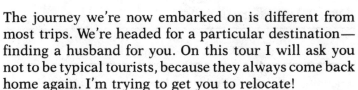

The journey we're now embarked on is different from most trips. We're headed for a particular destination—finding a husband for you. On this tour I will ask you not to be typical tourists, because they always come back home again. I'm trying to get you to relocate!

For you to get maximum advantage from your travels, I have to reiterate a point that I've already made. *You don't have any time to waste on the Mr. Wrongs out there.* The sightseeing is over. You're almost ready to venture into the land where the good men are, and live among the natives. Somewhere in that vast territory—if you can become a good enough explorer—there'll be a Mr.

Right-for-you. In fact, there should be several excellent candidates. First, you've got to get acclimated to the culture.

To stretch the travel analogy further is to remind you that before people go to live in foreign countries, they first study the culture as we did in Chapter 3. Then they talk to people who have a familiarity with the country. These people represent invaluable resources that are available *now*. Even after these resources have been utilized, however, there may still be important information gaps. One informant may say, for example: "You ought to talk to my friend, he/she has lived in the country longer than I have." Now your trail leads you to resource people who *you didn't know were available*. They may turn out to be more valuable than the ones you had firsthand. Any journey, whether to a strange country or toward a new goal, has a happier outcome if it is preceded by advance work.

In this chapter you're going to get some sample resource lists, with suggestions and comments about each item so that you can do a thorough job of compiling your own. The underlying assumption here is that you do need resources to find mates just as you do to find jobs, homes, and other vital necessities!

Available Resources

Friends—Sample 1

Friends (fill in names)	Have I told them I'm looking?	Have I asked if they are in a position to arrange some dates for me?	Do they know the kind of person I'm looking for?

_____	yes	no	no
_____	no	?	yes
_____	no	yes	no
_____	yes	yes	yes
_____	no	yes	no

It would be nice if you could fill in all the blanks with "yes," but you probably can't, so let's aim to get as many as you can. This will require some effort on your part.

More and more women are relying on their friends in order to meet men. Understandably, friends are the safest matchmakers since anyone they would introduce you to is someone they already know. Single female friends may match you with a man who didn't fit the bill for them, but it's unlikely that they'll pair you with a rapist! Whether married or single, friends presumably have, at the very least, your age and physical well-being in mind and, at most, your personality, tastes, and interests in mind when they arrange a match. I could leave the matter here except that I have made the startling discovery that women often don't inform their friends of their desire for blind dates and frequently neglect to ask them whether they know any available single men. Swallowing enough pride to get over these two hurdles is essential and should then enable you to give your friends a rough composite sketch of desirable men and a few characteristics to identify the undesirables. (Hopefully, the latter group consists of the Mr. Wrongs as identified in Chapter 3 with some additional allowances for _sensible_, subjective criteria for elimination, like _ethnicity_, if it's a major factor; _age_, if there's an unbridgeable gap; _smoking or nonsmoking_, if that's a big issue; _health_, if it's a serious enough problem, etc.)

Suffice it to say that friends are invaluable resource people. Without my friends, I can't imagine how I'd ever have gotten carpenters, plumbers, doctors, lawyers, a fair sampling of my own clients, as well as innumerable dates (when I was single). In order to reap the benefits, though, I did have to inform my friends that I was looking and whom I was looking for. On the slight chance that all of your friends are social isolates with little or no interaction with the outside world, I'd advise you to make new friends.

To hoist the banner for friends one last time, there's the story I got on the phone recently when talking to a successful female lawyer in Boston who is past the age of 40. "I had been single for 17 years until last year," she said. "I didn't want to take the risk of anonymous or chance encounters. When one of my good friends offered to introduce me to a man, I accepted on the basis of her recommendation. It wasn't a romantic jell at first, but we both persisted out of our mutual regard for her good opinion of us and our potential compatibility. Eight months later we got married. Not only was falling in love in middle age terrific, but we can't imagine how we ever considered not being married to one another."

Colleagues

Colleagues—Sample 2

Have I told them I'm looking?	Have I asked if they are in a position to arrange some dates for me?	Can I tell them I'm looking?

A) Co-workers

_____ _____ _____ _____

_____ _____ _____ _____

_____ _____ _____ _____

_____ _____ _____ _____

B) Colleagues
   in
   other
   offices
   whom I
   see
   regularly

_____ _____ _____ _____

_____ _____ _____ _____

_____ _____ _____ _____

_____ _____ _____ _____

Since a hefty proportion of your waking hours are spent at work, chances are that you and your colleagues are well acquainted, so why not think of them as good resources for your romantic pursuits? The questions about them are the same as those in Sample #1. Do they know you're looking for a mate? What single people do they know? Have you told them you'd like to be introduced to someone? Are they aware of the kinds of men you want to meet? You might even go a step further and ask them for their perceptions about you and potential mates for you. After all, they see you working and interacting on a daily basis. They are in a better position than most people in your network to observe your mannerisms, foibles, capabilities, and temperament. Why is it, then, that so many of you don't take *proper* advantage of these proximate relationships?

I think it's because your thinking gets fuzzy. You assume you're supposed to be "professional" at work and "personal" after hours. Some of you have become expert at "after-hours personal." The typical scenario has you going out at 5:30 for an innocent drink with your male colleague or boss (married or single—but very likely married), and at 8:30 you're at *your* apartment in bed together. By 10:00, he's left, and you're alone. Of course I know that there are many modifications and variations in the script, but the theme is always the same—office familiarity breeds SEX. Well, familiarity can breed a lot of encounters, but they don't all have to be sexual. In fact, the only appropriate time for sex to invade the collegial atmosphere is when two co-workers are *single and available and their relationship evolves into a romantic one.* I will elaborate on this in more detail in a later chapter.

We all bring our personal selves to the office, and there's really no need to draw such a hard line between our professional and personal selves. Sex is a poor and perilous tool with which to cross over the boundary. Open, honest, and direct communication yields much greater rewards. Putting this in concrete terms, let's take the commonplace example of the woman who's depressed because her romantic life is suffering. Everybody at work sees that she's depressed, but she doesn't say anything about it. She just plods along, but she's not much fun to have around. If she could share her feelings about what was bothering her with some of her trusted co-workers, and could solicit them as resources in the quest, she'd be doing herself and them a favor. Should she remain closed-mouthed, she's lost the opportunity for their input.

There's nothing inappropriate about revealing your personal needs to your professional colleagues as long as you're clear about your boundaries and discreet about your own behavior.

Groups

This item should give you an idea of your involvement in the world. It's begging for an answer to the question "Am I out there where I'm *visible* to people?" List the groups that you belong to, such as:

Groups—Sample 3

Clubs (Athletic, social, church) _____

_____

Organizations (Professional, political, religious) _____

_____

Interest Groups (Hobby-oriented activities) _____

_____

Classes (Adult education, university-affiliated) _____

_____

Social Groups (Singles, women's, dance, community) _____

_____

Others _____

_____

_____

If you don't belong to anything, how can you be seen?

Essential Resources That Are Presently Unavailable

In order to make a list of resources that you will need to acquire, you first have to go over the lists you just completed. Perhaps you discovered that you had enough people in your personal network who were in a position to assist you in your search for Mr. Right. Maybe you just hadn't realized it or had no knowledge of how to tap the oil well. If this is your situation, you're lucky. However, what is more probable is that you have some resources, but they are limited. Your friends, colleagues, and affiliations are not sufficient. They can be of some assistance to you, but you can't count on them to deliver you a mate.

Let's find out where the holes are on your list and then work on filling them in with additional supplies.

1. *Friends*—Sometimes friendships can be sources of support, encouragement, and direct assistance in helping us meet our needs. At other times, they can slow us down or bury us deeper in our ruts. If you have a tendency toward depression and an attitude of futility about love and life, one of the worst things you can do is to surround yourself with an assortment of like-minded people. Growing up means burning worn-out bridges. Some friendships do outlive their usefulness. I leave it to your good judgment to determine whether or not you have too many friends who reinforce your regressive side and not enough to validate your progressive side, but I'll come down strongly in favor of friendships that enhance your growth.

   Then there are those of you who don't have enough friends. For one reason or another you haven't cultivated friendships. Perhaps your own shyness, inflexibility, or passivity accounts for it. Social isolation tends to create romantic desperation. All your eggs go in the basket of finding one man to fill the gaping void, but as soon as he discovers that he is the only significant person in your life, he runs the other way. Not only does your isolation make you less vibrant and attractive to men, but it also keeps you out of circulation. As Maxine Schnall emphasizes in another of her books, *Every Woman Can Be Adored*, the three best ways for meeting eligible men are "contacts, contacts, contacts."* I couldn't agree more. Socially active friends are terrific contacts.

Then, there are those women who collect friends like philatelists collect stamps; they go everywhere in packs, as if to advertise that they outnumber men. If a man should approach one of them (which he has to be courageous to do), he's enveloped by the group. I'm all for female camaraderie, but there are times and places for it. Surely there's no worse time for a feminine klatch than when you're situated in an opportune setting for meeting eligible men. At every class that I've conducted where single men have been present, they have identified female groupiness as a significant deterrent.

2. *Colleagues*—Obviously, you can't throw over your colleagues if they're not supportive of you. That's up to your employer, and he or she has other things to consider besides your personal welfare. Likewise, it would be foolhardy to leave a good job because your co-workers were unable to enhance your love life.

There is, however, something to be said in favor of leaving jobs and colleagues when your self-

* Maxine Schnall, *Every Woman Can Be Adored* (New York: Coward-McCann, Inc., 1981), p. 70.

esteem is not enhanced by remaining on the job. When you derive personal satisfaction, recognition, and increasing maturity from your work, the effect is contagious. The confidence and pleasure you derive from your job spreads and enlivens your personality and your presence among people. So long as you prevent work and its rewards from becoming the essence of your life (at the expense of love), you have an advantage in the mating game.

We all know, though, that many people feel dissatisfied, trapped, and unappreciated in their jobs. Financial insecurity, fear of the unknown, the threat of joblessness, and family responsibilities combine to keep them at their desks. Here again, the effect is contagious and usually detrimental.

No question about it, single women who are unhappy at work are less attractive to men. Drudgery and dullness go hand in hand. If you're a discontented employee and if the fault lies with you, not the job, then you can act to improve your attitude and performance at work, but if it's the job, the work environment, or the co-worker incompatibility that is making you feel depressed and insignificant, then maybe you'll need to move on. Oh, I know what some of you will say: "How can I? I have two kids to support." "What? Give up my salary for no guarantee of anything comparable out there?" "When was the last time *you* looked for a job?" "Are you crazy? Don't you know there aren't any good jobs?" "My friend Sara has been looking for six months and still hasn't found one." I've heard it all before, but I'm persistent, and I use the same rebuttal every time: How badly do you want to find a good man? Are there ways that you can take the risk, minimize your losses, and come out ahead on the other end? (One obvious way is to get a new job *before* leaving the old one.) Are you better off if you're well paid and bored than you would be if you're slightly poorer and lively? Sure, it's hard to leave a secure position for an uncertain one. Whoever said that life was easy? Departures are part of living. We leave our original families, our friends, our communities, and even our former spouses. Sometimes we have to leave our jobs as well. Men do it all the time. Maybe there's a message there for us.

3. *Groups*—Suppose you don't belong to any social group. You're not a joiner. What effect does it have on your romantic fortunes? Possibly, if you're one of the lucky women who has plenty of friends and a supportive work environment, it won't matter that you're not a member of any civic or activity organization. I suspect, though, that the majority of you have learned that, however helpful your friends or colleagues may be, they have their own personal agendas to attend to. Like you, they are eager to find mates, and/or satisfying careers for themselves or, if married, they're preoccupied with familial concerns. Nowadays, people are very busy attempting to keep their own lives in order. It's no small achievement to keep a finger plugged into our own personal dikes. There are *limits* to what we can and are willing to do for each other. Eventually, we have to confront an inescapable reality: *We* have to do a lot for ourselves if we're going to get what we want out of life.

So what does all this have to do with joining clubs and organizations? The first and most obvious answer is that utilizing groups as resources for meeting men is one course of action that puts you in the driver's seat. You're *doing* something for yourself, and possibly for other people, too. Whatever you're doing reflects a *positive* feature of your character, whether it be athletic, academic, political, or otherwise.

From one of my own undocumented hunches

comes another, more subtle answer. I believe that *joining* groups brings a secondary psychological reward. Such groups release you, at least momentarily, from the *"poor-me syndrome."* The focus of organized groups is a single topic, activity, or interest, not a single person. While you're in attendance, you are enlisted to enjoy, participate, contribute, and/or listen, but the collective interests of the group override your own self-consciousness. Let's take hiking as an illustration. You may be a slower, less experienced hiker than some other members of the group, but in order to participate enjoyably, your attention needs to be focused on the hike rather than on your athletic liabilities. Group pressure in this context is a positive, dynamic force that tends to ignore your personal shortcomings and to highlight your best efforts. You don't need me to tell you, but I will anyway, that a woman with her best foot forward is an attractive woman to herself and to any prospective suitor who may be passing by.

There's another bonus to membership in groups that shouldn't go unmentioned. Again, it relates to the poor-me syndrome. Most groups demand some contribution from you. Seldom are rewards offered up without expectation of a payback. It's nobler to give than to receive, the Bible tells us, but what the Good Book doesn't say is that she who is a giver is more likely to be a receiver than she who thinks she is *entitled* to receive. If it is true that we are a generation of narcissists, always on the *take*, then group involvement is an opportunity to break out of the mold. We offer the best of ourselves to the common good.

At this point, you should know about the resources you have and those you will need. Make sure you can identify your existing resources and have located the gaps in them. I've given you some ideas about plugging up the holes, but you may want to add some thoughts of your own. You're going to need all these resources— and more—when you venture into husbandland. So we proceed.

In the next chapter, I'm going to send you out into the field alone without even waiting until you've had an opportunity to put your list of resources to the test. It's up to you to make use of your list as you go along. My job is to get you into husband territory right away— force you to get your feet wet. When guiding people through Paris, the best tour directors don't dump you off at the Eiffel Tower in the morning and pick you up at dinnertime. No, they take you at midday to quaint, little, out-of-the-way neighborhoods where you can wander by yourself and mingle with *the people*! That's just what I'm about to do, except that I'm not coming back to pick you up. Dress comfortably and look attractive, keep the inner you intact and your eyes wide open, and beware of Mr. Wrongs.

CHAPTER 5

Where Do I Go to Find Mr. Right?

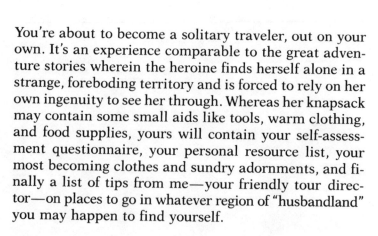

You're about to become a solitary traveler, out on your own. It's an experience comparable to the great adventure stories wherein the heroine finds herself alone in a strange, foreboding territory and is forced to rely on her own ingenuity to see her through. Whereas her knapsack may contain some small aids like tools, warm clothing, and food supplies, yours will contain your self-assessment questionnaire, your personal resource list, your most becoming clothes and sundry adornments, and finally a list of tips from me—your friendly tour director—on places to go in whatever region of "husbandland" you may happen to find yourself.

Dating Services

You probably know by now that I'm a proponent of dating services. I'm in favor of them because they fill a contemporary societal need: namely, to introduce single men and women to each other in a reasonably safe, legitimate, and convenient way. They exist because some farsighted business people have recognized that American life has become progressively more impersonal, transient, and technological. Given these trends, plus the rising divorce rate, dating services make good sense. If you're one of the lucky women who has a sizeable informal network of friends, acquaintances, and colleagues through whom you meet and date many men, then you may not need a dating service, but just suppose you aren't one of these fortunate women. (Don't worry, scores of women aren't!) Suppose instead that you're 35 or thereabouts. Maybe you're divorced or have always been single and let's say, for the fun of it, that you've recently moved from suburban Minneapolis, where you've resided for 10 years, to the center of Chicago, where you know very few people. You're ready for marriage and want to meet a man. What do you do? You *don't* wait until you've developed a circle of friends. That may take a while. You *don't* knock on your neighbor's door and ask him or her to introduce you to someone. Your neighbor may be unsavory. You *don't* approach your new boss, who you've only known for a week, to see if he or she has a supply of eligible men for you. (Once you and the boss are well acquainted you might, but now is not the time.) You *don't* hang out in bars where Mr. Wrongs are apt to be available in abundance. What do you do? You sign up with a *reputable* dating service. Even if you don't fit all the specifications above, but your romantic life is lagging, you sign up. What most women need and usually lack as a starter for locating Mr. Right is *volume*—numbers of men from whom to choose, as Tracy Cabot explains in her book, *How to Make a Man Fall in Love With You*.* Good dating services provide you with introductions to cross-sections of men.

There are several types of dating services on the urban-suburban market. Before providing you with a list of the types of dating services that are available, I'm going to offer you some tips that will make it easier for you to determine which services are right for you.

1. First, ask the price of membership, and then find out what you're getting for your money. Are you guaranteed a certain number of dates when you pay the initial fee, or does your membership run out in a defined time period whether or not any matches have been arranged? Some dating services don't offer any promises of match-ups.

2. Determine your budget in advance of any inquiries. Dating services can be costly, and in most instances you should be prepared to spend from $100 to $500 for a membership. Students in my classes who have never used dating services before are initially shocked at their cost, and then resentful of the intimation that "love" has become yet another consumer item. While I understand and sympathize with both points of view, I also feel obliged to prepare single women to face the *world as it is* instead of *the one they wish it were*. Nowadays, it is becoming increasingly apparent that women need to spend money to enhance their romantic prospects. For years, the total financial burden of dating and mating fell on men. Perhaps it's only fair that women now assume a share of the load. This all leads up to some strong financial advice:

* Tracy Cabot, *How to Make a Man Fall in Love With You* (New York: Dell Publishing Co., 1984).

Don't shortchange yourself or your love life by underspending to meet men, but don't go overboard and put yourself in debt for it, either.
3. Don't listen to other women's horror stories about dating services *unless they're specifically related to unethical management practices.* Most of the tales I've heard are variations on the "creeps" and "losers" theme, and they're not reliable. The "loser" Sally met when she joined is not the great guy Susie met at the same place, but you're acquainted with Sally and not with Susie. What you *don't* know can hurt you!
4. Use *discretion* and *good judgment* when you make a date through a dating service. It's a good idea to arrive independently for your first meeting, which should take place on neutral turf, i.e., a restaurant, theater, cocktail lounge, or other public facility, so that you get a chance to assess him in a safe environment.
5. Select the kinds of dating services that suit your style and your pocketbook from the following list.

Computer dating   These services usually ask you to apply by filling out an information sheet about yourself that is used as the basis for matching you with men whose personal data correlate with yours on the computer. You are then given a list of names of men you may wish to contact. Likewise, your name has been given to the men whose profiles match yours so that they can contact you as well. Computer dating services that have been in existence for a substantial period of time usually have a sizeable membership pool so that it is possible for you to receive a number of potential dates. The drawbacks to this method of matchmaking are that it is often impersonal and based on superficial criteria like similar hobbies, educational level, and ethnic background, which can be easily tabulated by a computer. Computer dating tends to be expensive. Your membership fee may entitle you to a fixed number of contacts or an unlimited number. Obviously, the latter arrangement is preferable.

Videodating This is an increasingly popular method of matchmaking. You make a videotape in which you describe yourself to a staff interviewer. Your tape is then made available to the staff to show to men who they feel might be compatible with you. Likewise, you are given the opportunity to see tapes of men. No names or phone numbers are exchanged until you and a man (or men) have mutually agreed that you want to meet. The obvious advantage of videodating is that you have already seen the men you're going to meet and vice versa, so that some screening has taken place before you get together. Because you have a role in the selection process, the matches are more apt to be to your liking than they might be with other types of dating services. Videodating can be especially rewarding if you happen to be a person who projects well on screen. It's terrific for someone who is physically attractive and reasonably poised and articulate. It is costly, though, both in time and in money. You will need some spare hours to view the tapes and enough spare cash to part with the $300 to $500 it will cost to join.

Specialized dating services

There are a myriad of other kinds of dating services that are designed to appeal to particular groups of people. Cities that have large singles populations are apt to offer a wide range of choices. If you happen to fall into one of the categories listed below, you might do well by joining one or more of the specialized services. Often, these are less expensive than the computer and videodating services.

Ethnic or religious dating services In some cities, there are dating services that cater exclusively to certain ethnic or religious groups, i.e., blacks, Jews, Catholics. Some of these groups have national memberships.

"Yuppie" dating services   Some dating services concentrate their efforts on mating college-educated, professional male and female clientele.

Mid-life and older dating services   Some matchmaking entrepreneurs have recognized that there are legions of divorced men and women over 40 who are looking for mates. Such services attempt to make matches among this group of people.

Overweight dating services   Yes, there are even dating services in some cities that cater to people who are overweight so that they can meet each other and avoid possible embarrassment. Some of these are national organizations.

Handicapped dating services   One such organization is called Handicap Introduction (telephone [213] 282-1577). At this writing, it is the only dating service of its kind that I've heard about.

Other Dating Services

Bumper-sticker dating services   A relatively new phenomenon, these bumper-sticker matches are arranged while you're in the driver's seat. With a little bit of luck, as you wend your way through traffic, you may spot a car with an attractive driver and a conspicuous membership decal. You call the central office to find out who he is. First, you must join, if you aren't already a member, and then you get information about the man you saw whose decal number you carefully recorded. If you want to meet him, you can contact him. Once you're sporting the club decal on your car, other men may ask to meet you, as well.

Lunchtime dating services   In Boston, where I live, there are now two of these popular dating services that require you to join by submitting a personality profile. Next, you are matched with prospective men with whom you can arrange lunch dates. These services are attractive to people with limited time who like the idea of brief meetings during lunch hour.

National and international dating services   There are dating services that hook up matches across state, country, and continental lines. These may be especially helpful to people who live in areas where there are few single people and limited matchmaking resources.

. . . . .

I haven't begun to cover all the dating-service possibilities there are, but I hope I've impressed upon you the fact that they exist in abundance. Some of them are cheap enough to enable you to join several simultaneously. To start, all you need to do is run your finger through the Yellow Pages of your local phone directory. For another good listing of dating services and other singles resources in the United States and Canada (with an abundance of updated information), I recommend that you also get a copy of Carolyn Mordecai's useful book *Finding Love in the '80s* (Nittany Press, 1984). To receive a copy, mail a check for $5.95 to Nittany Press, Box 702, State College, PA 16804.

Now, I'm going to move from the dating services to one of my favorite singles resources, personal ads.

Personal Ads

Personal ads appeal to my sense of adventure. If I were single, at any age, but especially at mine (40 plus) I'd place ads in as many publications as I could afford.

All you have to do is write up a *clever, honest, brief,* well-constructed description of yourself and send it off— with a check, of course—to your favorite publications (some of which are listed in Carolyn Mordecai's book) and then watch your post office box fill up. Or, if you prefer, you can answer ads that men have placed, and you'll still see some activity in your post office box. I think if I were you, I'd do both. Who doesn't like to get a lot of personal mail?

There is a trick to writing personal ads so that they are intriguing to readers. They have to capture your uniqueness. If your ad sounds like everybody else's, and gives no solid clues about your individuality, it's likely to go unnoticed. Here are two examples of personal ads— one bad, the other good:

Bad Ad

"42 year old, childless, WDF (white, divorced female), *attractive, intelligent, fun-loving* professional desires long-term relationship with a 40–55 year old WM (white male) who is *good-looking, intelligent, fun,* and *successful* and likes theatre, dining out and walks in the country."

This ad is loaded with meaningless words. How is she attractive? What kind of intelligence does she have? And, what kind of fun-loving does she love? Who *doesn't* like good-looking, intelligent, fun, successful men, and what are *her* definitions of these vague adjectives? Show me a woman who doesn't like dining out, going to the theatre, and walking in the country and I'll tell her that she's one in a million! The only specific, clear information in this ad is that the writer is white, divorced, 42, childless, and desires a man in a particular age range who might want to hang around for a while.

Good Ad

"42 year old, childless WDF—a well-proportioned, petite, 5'3" blonde, energetic, high school teacher—wishes to share her enthusiasm for photography, journeys to exotic, out-of-the-way places, many sports, and program viewing on public television with a 40–50 year old man who has no worrisome vices, likes his work, respects women, and takes a lively interest in all kinds of activities. He needn't be Don Juan, just pleasant to look at, but he should be ready and willing to entertain the notion of marriage if our "fit" is good. If he has kids, that's fine, too."

Don't you like her a lot better now than you did in her first ad? Need I say more?

After you've composed your *good* ad, you mail it to whatever national, international, or local publications you think have the kind of readers who would interest you. By way of encouragement, I'll tell you about a divorcée I know who moved to Boston at age 43, with two teen-agers. Before she had gotten around to placing her own ad, she responded to an inventive one written by a man in a weekly advertiser. That was over a year ago. They're going so strong that she never did submit one of her own!

The moral of the personal-ad story is: make your ad as *specific* as you can. Be *honest*; don't say you're gorgeous unless you really are, or that you're mild-mannered if you're volatile, or athletic if you're sedentary. Describe your physical self *accurately*. If you're naturally *witty*, make your ad reflect it. Identify your job classification and your religious and political affiliations if they are germane to your romantic interests. *Avoid* the hackneyed words of the 1980s: "youthful," "sensitive," "intelligent," "fun-loving," "successful," "attractive."

So much for personal ads. They're fun to write, and the answers you receive are even more fun.

Singles Organizations

Every large city has clubs or organizations for single people. Some clubs have central themes like travel, books, music, etc. Others are social groups. Among them there are a number that are national in scope. I can't name them all here, but I can give you an overview. Again, Carolyn Mordecai's book offers a sampling of many of them with phone numbers and addresses:

1. Single parents: Parents Without Partners, a national organization with branches in major cities, catering to single parents and children, offering a variety of educational and social activities.
2. Singles travel clubs.
3. Singles groups under religious auspices.
4. Singles clubs for college-graduate professionals.
5. Singles clubs for high-income people.
6. Singles book and music clubs (see Mordecai's book).
7. Ethnic singles clubs.
8. Singles social clubs (a wide variety).

Some Organizations Not Exclusively for Single People—but Good Meeting Places

1. Appalachian Mountain Club—hiking, skiing, walking, camping, etc.
2. Ski clubs.
3. Health and athletic clubs. Many of these have activities designed for single people.
4. Photography, book, and/or music clubs.
5. Audubon Society—birdwatching.
6. Political and special-interest organizations—

American Civil Liberties Union (ACLU), Democratic and Republican party (local headquarters), National Association for the Advancement of Colored People (NAACP), Young Americans for Freedom (YAF), gun control organizations, nuclear disarmament organizations, organizations aiding Jewish causes, pro- and anti-abortion groups, TransAfrica (anti-apartheid group).

Adult-Education Classes

This is another of my favorite resources, probably because I teach them, and I've seen firsthand that single people can and do make connections there. Classes are comfortable, easy, un-self-conscious settings for men and women to get together. Unconsciously, adult-education classes may take us back to adolescence, when we began to make connections with the opposite sex, i.e., "the boy who sat next to me in algebra" or "the cute one who looked at me in homeroom." Sometimes, we dated those boys, or went "steady" with them, or even married them. In those halcyon days, endless possibilities for love lurked in classrooms, corridors, and libraries.

Single people are flocking to adult-education classes. They have a reputation for respectability, as places where "nice" people come to learn something. They also come to meet someone of the opposite sex, if luck is with them. There's none of the meat market ambience that is characteristic of singles bars and certain singles functions.

It's not a bad idea to sign up for classes that attract men, so long as you are genuinely interested in the subject matter. Classes that are reputed to draw men are investment and finance, real estate, photography, computers, and all manner of psychology and self-improvement classes.

The Office

I'm not a member in good standing of the keep-love-out-of-the-office club. On the contrary, I think it's a natural and very likely setting in which to meet Mr. Right. Let's face it, we all spend so much time there, and if *available* men happen to be on the premises, chances are you're going to know some of them well. It's very possible, too, that you just might find one you're sort of sweet on. Is it realistic for you then to put on a suit of armor and ward him off in order to pay homage to some vague standard of professional comportment? What you do need to do is keep your head screwed on while your heart is beating! Don't do your lovemaking in his office or yours, and don't allow your feelings for each other to hurt your productivity. Managing love with someone at work requires discipline, self-control, and discretion, but most of you are equal to this task. Countless long-term relationships, my own included, have sprung from, and are maintained in, the office. No corporate policy should stop people from doing what comes naturally. But single women can and should have a strict policy about doing what comes illicitly—dating married colleagues. *Don't do it.* Put that at the top of your list of restrictions in your personal office manual.

Other Places to Go and Things to Do

- *Restaurants*—If you have enough self-confidence to dine alone.
- *Bars*—If they're reputable and you have very good judgment and an ability to decline more offers than you accept.
- *Vacations*—If you can feel comfortable traveling alone, and you've selected a place where you really want to be.

- *Stores, buses, planes, trains, and lobbies*—If you have the gift of gab and an accurate, discriminating eye.
- *Parties*—If you're good at small talk, don't suffer from painful shyness, and can play the pursuer as well as the pursued.
- *Art galleries and openings*—If you like modern art, and the kind of people who like it.

· · · · ·

At last I've gotten you out into the field where men have been waiting to be found. My next job is to help you help yourself, if these resources are inadequate to the task.

CHAPTER 6

Building Networks

In the preceding chapter, I put you out in the field, where you will remain for a while longer. Having taken this trip many times before, both personally and professionally, I know what to expect. Some of you will jump on the bandwagon, take my suggestions, and implement them in practice. Others of you will be resistant and will find excuses for doing nothing, telling yourselves that it isn't "natural" for you to do these things to meet men. (Let me remind you that nothing is "natural" until you try it and learn to do it.) Still others of you will sample my prescriptions, and find that the medicine isn't providing the remedy you had hoped for. To those of you

who do take my advice to heart, a precaution is in order:
It all takes *time*. If right away you don't succeed in finding HIM, do keep on trying. This business of husband
hunting is not an overnight happening. It's a process that
takes place over time.

Now that you've had a chance to acclimate, there's
something else you may need to do in addition to trying
dating services, personal ads, singles groups, etc. It's a
way of meeting men that deserves a chapter of its own.
At this moment, it's a nonexistent resource for you,
but you can create it with a little ingenuity and assertiveness. Nowadays, they call this particular resource
a *network*. In actuality, networks are a more structured replacement for what people claim they came by
naturally in the good old days, i.e., families, friends,
neighbors, and workmates functioning informally as
connecting links between each other and on behalf of
one another.

Obviously, our huge, mobile, fast-paced 1980s society
can't bring back this folksy togetherness (if in fact it ever
existed), but no one questions that connecting links are
more vital than ever to help hook us up to people, jobs,
institutions, homes, and services. Without networks, it's
easy to feel like the lost wanderer in an endless desert.
While not applicable to everything in life, the old adage
"It's not *what* you know, but *who* you know that counts"
makes good sense for women needing to meet men.

To begin building a network, you need to take out your
personal "who I know" resource list of friends, colleagues, and acquaintances and combine it with the resources I provided for you in the last two chapters. How
can you convert all or some of these resources into a
mate-finding network? Instead of answering the question directly, I'm going to come at it indirectly by telling
you about a special feature of the "Mating Game" classes
that I conduct at the Boston Center for Adult Education,
as well as at selected classes and workshops that I do

elsewhere. I make the assumption at the outset of each new class that participants have been motivated to enroll for two reasons: 1) to learn about the topic, 2) to meet eligible men and women. At this point in time, I'm so sure of the second assumption that I don't even verify it anymore. Routinely, a portion of the final class session is addressed to this assumption. Students are asked to meet for 15 to 30 minutes without benefit of my leadership in order to form a cooperative network to help each other meet mates. The only requirement is that someone act as secretary and record all names and phone numbers as well as the kind of network the group has decided to form. The appointed secretary copies the list and sends it to everyone. I receive a copy as well as a report on the kind of network the group decides to establish.

There are three premises that underlie the requirement. The *first* is the premise that even if there are no potential matches within the group itself due to age differences, imbalance between male and female, social class, racial, cultural, or other gaps, these people represent resources for each other. *Second* is the premise that if this moment is not seized as an opportunity, it will be lost, hence each member of the group will have passed up a chance to meet *someone through knowing everyone. Third* is the premise that there just might possibly have been the potential for a match or two within the group, but that for one reason or another it didn't get off the ground while the class was still on. The network provides second looks and chances.

Because many of you will not have the benefit of a structured class to start the network, you will need to do the initiating yourself. This is done by contacting friends, colleagues, and acquaintances who then repeat the same procedure with the people they know. Living rooms in different people's homes are ideal meeting places.

After five years of teaching, my file bulges with names and networks. Here I will describe the prototypes that have been developed.

Share-the-Wealth Network

A group forms with an even distribution of men and women for the purpose of a party or series of parties to which invited guests agree to bring a *friend* of the opposite sex with whom he or she is not romantically involved. In some instances, group discussions or lectures are held instead of parties with time for mingling after the program. Whatever the form is, there is the stipulation that you must bring someone in order to attend.

Referral Networks

These groups can be exclusively female and can spread over a wide age range. People meet, get to know one another, and learn as much as they can about each other's mate preferences. Then, each person thinks of all the available men she knows and agrees to attempt to arrange blind dates between the group members and men on her list. If a group meets often enough, there is opportunity for sharing information about the effectiveness of the referral process, discussion on individual dating experiences, and feedback between members about personal attitudes and behaviors that may be preventing a person from reaching her goal—finding a mate. The referral network requires a commitment, but it functions effectively over time. Its advantage is that it acts as a built-in support group and can result in close and lasting friendships as well.

Pass-Him-On Network

When first presented, this idea meets with hilarious resistance. Jokes about garbage-picking, hand-me-downs, and reject piles are the typical responses. Once the comedic atmosphere quiets down, however, the idea becomes less preposterous. If women concentrate on *why* they've dated and then rejected certain men, they discover that often it's been because of religion, ethnic background, physical characteristics, stature, age, career interest, number of children, etc. The parting of such company is not always accompanied by animosity. It's well within the realm of possibility that someone who wasn't right for you might be a good bet for someone in your network. The way it works is that a group of women gather *once* and get each other's names, addresses, and phone numbers, pertinent personal information, and identifying data about desirable men. After that, it's a matter of contacting your old beau (or male friends as in the referral network) to see if they're game for meeting new women. If the reply is affirmative, you give him the woman's number and then let her know that you have done so.

The advantage of this kind of network over the referral type is that it's less time-consuming. I've been told that if you have an *assertive, energetic, enthusiastic* group of women, it works very well, so you might want to select your group with these qualifications in mind.

Resource Networks

These are information-sharing networks that have proved very popular with my classes. They're easy to organize, require only a small time investment, and are appealing to groups with diversity among their members. Meetings can be held two to four times a year.

People gather to share resources and experiences with one another. Because new singles activities, establishments, and services crop up regularly on the metropolitan horizon, a resource network can be a useful method for keeping abreast of the latest, "hottest" tips on where to go and what to do to meet members of the opposite sex. It also provides an opportunity for people to report on resources they've tried and how well they've been served.

Single people are eager for resource information, so this network goes a long way toward satisfying that appetite. I wouldn't recommend it for people who are seeking support and direct matchmaking from a group. Resource networks are loosely organized, noncommittal, and easily disbandable. They deliver *information*, and if that's what you want, then they're right for you. A word of warning: You can be certain that there will be one or more doomsayers in the midst of a resource network, and they are often the very people who are most knowledgeable about the resources. Keep one ear open for the resources, and the other closed to the doomsaying.

Exclusive Networks

You can form networks around ethnic affiliations, social class considerations, age groups, interests, etc. In large cities, dating entrepreneurs and special-interest clubs provide these services, usually for a fee. Dating services, personal ads, singles organizations, and singles clubs are authentic networks but they're in existence to make a profit. They have to be accessible to you geographically and financially, and they don't pretend to provide the intimacy of the living-room networks mentioned here.

Here, I'm going to talk about networks with which I have no personal familiarity. In fact, many of them probably don't exist anywhere, but I have a firm conviction that they should.

A regrettable but very real feature of our society is its social stratification. We live by the principle of exclusivity. You're well educated; I'm not, so we're not friends. You're black; I'm white, so we won't have anything in common. You're a laborer; I'm an executive, so we don't mingle. You're handicapped; I'm not, so I probably have never even known you. You're 72; I'm 35, so what would we have to talk about?

Our stereotypes rule us and set the permanent stage for our social lives. Most of our adulthood is spent in compartmentalized, homogeneous niches with clearly marked boundary lines: "Don't cross over if you don't belong."

Much as I might like to tear down social fences (and in my own life I have), I'm a realist, and I admit my inability to change the social fabric. Furthermore, the highest and most indestructible fences are built around the mating field, so that I can't have much influence there either—expertise notwithstanding.

Thus, the networks I'm about to propose (for mating purposes only) are based on the acknowledgment, albeit grudging, of the reality of social and romantic exclusivity.

1. *Nonprofessional People's Networks*

    Although many dating services accept applications from people in all job classifications, prices in many are high enough to exclude lower-salaried people. To compound this dilemma, a hefty percentage of highly educated, professional men are seeking women of the same stripe. Thus, I have concluded that there is a big need for moderately priced, nonprofessional video and computer dating services and no-cost networks targeted to this segment of the singles population.

2. *Educated Black People*

    As mentioned previously, black women in this category are up against the odds. There are not enough professional black men to go around, certainly not in one locality. Thus, the "go national" idea is compelling. One or more national dating networks for professional black men and women should be established, with the simultaneous advancement, through advertising and publicity, of the long-distance romance concept.

3. *Minority Networks*

Far too many minority men and women of all educational backgrounds are excluded from the singles mainstream, either for economic reasons or for more obvious ones like racism, psychological barriers, cultural differences, etc. Minority women have a shallow pool (if, in fact, they have one at all) to choose from in the profit-making, dating marketplace. Most cities could use many more minority singles' networks, either for profit or not, than presently exist. As it now stands, minority men and women appear reluctant to utilize services that cater primarily to whites. While it is a mistake for them not to inquire about these resources because some do arrange minority/minority or minority/nonminority matches, there will be large numbers of people who will never contact a white-operated network.

4. *Handicapped People's Network*

As I mentioned in the preceding chapter, there is one national dating network for the handicapped. It is the only one, to my knowledge. Local singles networks for handicapped people are badly needed.

5. *45-and-Over People's Network*

The rising divorce rate leaves many people single after the age of 45. For women, this constitutes a serious problem, because they outnumber available men in a much higher proportion than they do in the younger years, and there are fewer available matchmaking resources for them. Furthermore, as has been widely publicized, a percentage of age-level men remarry younger women. Despite these obstacles, there are available men in the 45-and-over age group for whom the youth-oriented singles scene is not appropriate or desirable. Many a mid-life woman has been discouraged from joining singles services for lack of male membership in her age range. Networks for older single people are in such short supply that if several were established in any major city, it's unlikely that they would go begging for applicants, though there would undoubtedly be fewer men than women.

6. *Special-Interest Networks*

Having dealt with networks geared to ethnic, social class, and age considerations, I'll expand the idea into the "special interests" field. Already on the horizon, there are a large number of organizations, some exclusively for single people, that revolve around specific activities or interests. I am speaking to single women who have "interests" that might better be called "passions." They love to read, jog, ski, swim, play tennis, or listen to music, and life without regular involvement in one or more such "passions" would be barren. Why not form your own singles network around a passionate interest, if your geographic area doesn't provide one or if the existing ones are too large, too impersonal, or too expensive for your tastes? Building this kind of a network is a manageable and relatively easy task to perform. You can start with a base of friends, colleagues, and acquaintances as described in some of the examples in this chapter, or you can place an ad in a local newspaper, magazine, or publication with a singles readership.

In summary, building a network to meet a man is like purchasing a "do-it-yourself kit" to build anything. What this method costs in time, it saves in money, and there is nothing quite like the rewarding feeling you get when you gaze at the finished product! Just try to imagine what your efforts could potentially yield on the romantic front!

. . . . .

If luck is with me, these last two chapters have planted us securely on an "action" track. In order to insure that the activity remains productive, we will take a time-out from it to participate in a "reflective" experience.

CHAPTER ⫻ 7

How to Be Your Own Worst Enemy in Love: The Seven Most Common Love Traps

If I felt confident that your journey would proceed smoothly, I would have ended our tour at the last chapter and bid you farewell and good luck. But I know how perilous this journey can be, so I'm sticking with you for a while longer. In fact, we're about to reunite for a seminar. *Sabotage*—all the things you can do to hurt your own chances for success in love—is the topic for the first portion of our meeting. There are any number of traps that you can set for yourself along the way, but if I warn you in advance about them, maybe I can save you valuable time and freedom from heartache. I know that most of you are accustomed to thinking of "traps"

95

as devices that somebody else (in this case, a man) sets for you to fall into, but it is my conviction that for every romantic trap that's set there are two culprits—a man and a woman—and the victim is every bit as responsible for the "fall" as the oppressor is. Because women so often see themselves as the *victims* of the trap, they are prone to overlook their own culpability.

How do these traps get set? How do you identify them? How do you avoid falling into them?

How the Traps Get Set: Daddy

None of us had perfect fathers and, according to Dr. William Appleton, author of *Fathers and Daughters*, this is a mixed blessing. Daddies have to be knocked off their pedestals in order for us to move on to successful relationships with lovers and husbands. The problem, as Appleton points out, is not that fathers have to fall in our esteem, but rather how gradually or severely they do so.* For example, if we have had distant, stern, absent, overprotective, overly attentive, abusive, or seductive fathers, the fall is apt to be severe and can leave us with damaging scars. On the other hand, if our fathers were appropriately available, gentle, admiring, and encouraging and could accept our recognition of their imperfections, the fall is more gradual. Then, we will have an easier time giving up our love affairs with Dad and advancing into happy adult relationships. Because so many of us have been trained about men at the knees of the first order of Daddies and not the second, it is incumbent upon us to understand that our accumulated experience with fathering does have an effect on our behavior with men. We are ripe for the wrong pickings

* William Appleton, M.D., *Fathers and Daughters* (New York: Berkley Books, 1984), p. 17.

and conversely very adroit at picking rotten fruit or finding no fruit at all! Not only do we ignore the powerful effects of our father's influence, but we also forget that the men in our lives had Mommies, some of whom weren't so hot, either. To make matters worse, a lot of men don't have the slightest inkling that their relationships with Mom are still haunting them in their adult love lives.

The moral of the story, and it's a moral for every woman, especially those who had difficult relationships with their fathers: *Make yourself consciously aware of your relationship with your father. Dredge up every memory, however painful, of life with (or without) Father. Force yourself, with the help of a therapist, if you need to, to examine his impact on you and yours on him, and keep your new knowledge in the forefront of your mind.* If you have not already done so, you will have to make some kind of peace between you and your Dad. If you don't, the price can be very high indeed. It can cost unnecessary divorce, damaged children, loveless married or unmarried lives, and a host of chronic psychological and physical complaints. This is not to say that you can't or won't make mistakes. You will and you must, because that is how all of us grow, but some mistakes are worse than others. Better to make a lot of small ones than a few disastrous ones. I'm not implying that all divorces should be viewed as disasters, but certainly some of them are, and a hefty proportion of those could have been avoided had "she" understood more about "Dad" and "he" understood more about "Mom." The awareness gives each of them *choices* about behaving differently. Without it, there are no choices.

To close this section on a more optimistic note, let me reassure you that if you're willing to expend the time and energy to reopen the book between you and Dad (if need be) and then to alter your inappropriate adult behaviors, there are dividends to be reaped. Having seen well over 100 female clients in my private practice, I have their personal biographies as evidence that Daddy makes his presence (or absence) felt. *Nobody, not any man, can make up for what you didn't get from him!* You're going to have to come to terms with whatever paternal disappointments you have suffered. Don't expect compensation to be paid by one man or a string of men.

Here are some of the traps that you are likely to fall into as a result of unfinished business with Daddy:

The "Perfect Man" Trap

There are women (not as many as one might think, though) who go on endless expeditions to locate the perfect man. They pass up all the "imperfect" men in search of this phantom of perfection. The fantasy feels something like this: "He will be a composite of *all* my favorite male characteristics. He's going to be Mr. Everything, and he will know how to make me feel that I'm Mrs. Everything. He will look just *right*, behave just *right*, perform just *right*, and treat me *right*." (She knows what *right* is, it's just that she hasn't found it.) Her standards are so high that nobody can attain them. The men who have the best chance of coming closest to the mark are "the rats," as described by Drs. Cowan and Kinder in *Smart Women, Foolish Choices*.* These are the men who have made a lifetime habit of studying women, and have mastered the art of tantalizing and enthralling them in order to satisfy their own egos, but they're men who never let down their charming guards enough to genuinely love women (whether or not they marry). The pursuit of the rat—the man who skillfully masquerades as Mr. Everything—leads to inevitable disappointment.

Women in search of perfect men are hungry women, and the *quest* to satisfy their appetites is more intriguing and exciting than the *actual satisfaction. Hunger* and *love* are synonymous in their heads. They value most what

---

* Dr. Connell Cowan and Dr. Melvyn Kinder, *Smart Women, Foolish Choices* (New York: Clarkson N. Potter, 1985), pp. 76 & 77.

they can't have. Some never give up the hunt, but the lucky ones get exhausted and recognize that they are living on perpetually empty stomachs, so they change course and fill up on a diet of love with splendid but imperfect men.

In defense of women, I must explain that the media are very fond of "the perfect man" theme, and it gets considerable play in print and on radio and TV talk shows. It is now part of the conventional wisdom to assume that women who are still involuntarily single are in that sorry state because they're looking for perfection in men. From my experience, the evidence is not out there to support this thesis. Looking for Mr. Perfect, while certainly a problem for some women, is far from being the major cause of unwanted female singledom. Only a handful of the hundreds of women I meet in my classes and in private practice appear to me to be seeking perfection in men. I don't believe that it is the primary trap. Today's women are too psychologically sophisticated to fall into it en masse, but there are still some who do, and it is to that small minority that this lesson has been addressed.

The "Chemistry" Trap

This is the trap that trips so many women. Pity that the media don't give *it* the attention it deserves. I'd be very wealthy now if I'd been paid every time I'd heard a woman say, after meeting a new man, "He's nice, but I'm just not attracted to him." Women harbor some crazy expectation that the juices and adrenalin should start flowing almost immediately upon meeting a man. They tell themselves that they should feel a thrilling rush — a volcano should erupt inside them causing shaking at the knees, limpness in the arms, and loud heart throbbing! Then they'll know that he's the one. Had I married every man with whom I'd experienced this exhilarating "chemical reaction," I'd have had many husbands by now instead of only one. The "chemistry" factor boils down to a basic principle: The sudden surge of passion is no indication of anything beyond a pleasurable sensation at the moment (or moments) when it occurs, and the onset of that moment can come at any time in a relationship. It does not have to be *instantaneous*. It can evolve, and definitely will diminish in intensity soon after it begins. There are no rules about when "chemistry" should occur, and its appearance doesn't provide any clues about a man as a potential mate. (From listening to women, I have come to the opinion that the chemistry that builds gradually is more indicative of a potentially successful relationship than the chemistry that starts with an explosion. The former seems to me to be connected to the mates having progressed to the level of knowing each other. Their attraction then has a measure of intimacy as a base.) The existence of "chemistry" is merely testimony to the fact that there is a physical attraction between you and him. *That's all!* At this point, I can anticipate your response. You won't like what I've said, and you'll be fighting me in your head. I've got a rebuttal ready for you. Yes, physical attraction is great fun, even thrilling, and *at many points* in a relationship I would want you to experience it, because it is one of the great "highs" that nature provides us. BUT you shouldn't hang your romantic fate on the delusion that if it isn't there on the first date or even the 15th date that it won't ever appear. It can creep up at the most unexpected times, and it's pure foolishness to pass someone by because it isn't there just when you want it to be. If you lead with your *head* in love, your *heart* will usually follow, but if you lead with your heart, it's easy to lose your head. From there, it's a short hop into the trap. Dr. Carol Cassell wrote an entire book on this phenomenon in women. She called it *Swept Away*,* and the title tells the story. The delusional aura of chemistry, the

* Carol Cassell, Ph.D., *Swept Away*, (Simon and Schuster, New York, 1984).

need to surround it with more significance than it deserves, has tripped up many a woman and swept her into a bottomless pit.

The "Patterns" Trap

Drs. Yehuda Nir and Bonnie Maslin, in their book *Loving Men for All the Right Reasons*, do an excellent job of explaining, illustrating, and helping women to correct their self-destructive romantic patterns. Patterns are defined as unfruitful *repetitive* experiences that keep reappearing in a woman's romantic biography.* All of us who have been engaged in the practice of psychotherapy with women (and men, for that matter) are familiar with these nagging patterns. Always they spring, as the authors point out, from some *unconscious* need accompanied by a conflicting *conscious* wish.† The *wish* might be as simple as "I want to be married" but the *need* might compel her to repeatedly share a man with another woman. The woman who is caught in this particular pattern trap is the familiar one who has had countless relationships with married or single men who have another lover (or lovers) in the wings. Every relationship finds her hanging on to win her prize—victory over the other woman—but she never wins and each loss only sets her off in the same circular pattern again.

The above description pertains to just *one* of the many repetitive, self-defeating patterns that women employ to keep their wishes from coming true. In order to determine whether or not you're stuck in a pattern, you should *first* review your romantic history in the following order: 1) Did you experience frequent disappointment or confusion in your relationship with your father, or an ex-

---

* Yehuda Nir, M.D., and Bonnie Maslin, Ph.D., *Loving Men for All the Right Reasons* (New York, Dell Publishing Co., 1982), pp. 6 & 7.

† Ibid., p. 13.

cessively strong attachment to him? 2) Do you *repeatedly* lose at love? 3) Is there a certain type of man who unfailingly captures your interest? 4) Do you feel that you're incomplete without a man? 5) Do you reject most men who demonstrate a genuine fondness for you? If you answered "yes" to all of these questions, the chances are good that a pattern is controlling your romantic behavior. If you answered "yes" to some, but not all, these are danger signals for you to heed to avoid a pattern. (I see many women in their twenties who are heading into a pattern but have not yet arrived. That's the very best age for a therapist to intervene because a lot of pain can be prevented. Nonetheless, I've seen just as many women who've already been wounded by longstanding patterns. When they're motivated, they can and do break out.)

The "Dependency" Trap

To ascertain whether or not you are a good candidate for the dependency trap, listen attentively to your own telltale mutterings. "*I can't live* without him." "I *need* him." "Without him, my life would be *meaningless*." "We are *inseparable*." All of these phrases illustrate "dependency" but are intended to connote "love," as if the two words were interchangeable. "Dependency" in this context smacks more of addiction than of love. Stanton Peele, in *Love and Addiction*, describes the love addict as one whose attachment to another person serves as a replacement for appreciating and coping with the environment or with herself or himself. The so-called loved one is thus relied upon as the source of gratification—the person *through* whom to derive substance, security, sustenance, satisfaction, and escape from selfhood.* The love addict's theme song could be entitled "*I'm Hooked on You.*"

Real adult love is an *addition* to life, like a salary

---

* Stanton Peele, *Love and Addiction* (New York: Signet Books, 1975), p. 56.

bonus, rather than like the salary on which one's economic survival is predicated. Grown-up, nonaddictive lovers sing "I get a kick out of you, but I don't have to count on you for all my kicks, 'cause I can also get a kick out of life, work, my hobbies, interests, and myself."

Men who are overtly and covertly expected to "take care of and take charge of" women grow weary eventually. Love is a job rather than a pleasure, and the man who *chooses* to work this tiring second shift is inviting premature aging. Gradually, he's drained of vitality.

Oftentimes, dependency operates in the reverse. He chooses *you* to be his caretaker-spouse. At first, it can make you feel self-important. He *needs* you, so your ego is inflated. Only *you*—the one rose in a forest of thorns— can do it. How could any one woman be so *special*? She *can't*! The sooner she recognizes that *her* self-esteem can't be bought with *his* needs, the better her chances to break out of the dependency trap.

Confusing dependency for love is tantamount to installing an unpluggable drain in your life that rids you of energy, vitality, and sexuality.

The "Success" Trap

Often after one of my classes, I go to sleep at night with a chorus of female voices ringing in my ears. They are telling me that "he must be successful, must make more money than they do, be able to support them." Sometimes these voices keep me awake. Has the world gone mad, I ask myself, or is it me? What happened to the fervor of women's liberation? Have we returned full circle to the mentality of the '50s when women had to be "supported" by their spouses? Most of the women I've just heard are self-supporting, bona fide members of the professional class. They are financially independent and wouldn't dream of abandoning their hard-won careers, but still they *want* to be supported. For them, Mr. Right wears a three-piece suit and brings home more bags of bacon than they do, more than they'll ever need. So why do they talk like this? Some of it, I can blame on their mothers who were married in an "unliberated" era, and impressed on their daughters the notion that the selection of a husband was as much a financial matter as a romantic one. (Good psychotherapists know that mothers' words can command more staying power than the rhetoric of political movements!) Ironically, I can blame the rest of it on their misguided ideas about "romance" as symbolized by the prevalent fantasy of finding a man "I can *lean* on." The macho image of "big" and "strong" has gone out of fashion. Now, "big" and "strong" means "rich." Never mind if he's a wimp, if *he's* rich, *she's* protected!

After a few sleepless nights, I concluded that these women were deluding themselves and that my best offense was to confront them with cold, hard reality. I'll do the same for you.

In the 1982 U.S. census statistics, the *mean* (average) income for managerial and professional positions in the United States was $39,343 a year. For technical, sales, and administrative positions, it was $28,048 a year. Having previously documented the existence of an American man shortage, it doesn't take much ingenuity to recognize that when you are combining the overall man shortage with the *rich* man shortage, the statistics don't add up in favor of landing a wealthy man. If you use a man's high income as an essential criterion for his suitability as a mate, you are inviting disappointment. There aren't nearly enough such men to go around, and among those who are available, a certain percentage will have to be ruled out for reasons of character. It just doesn't make good romantic sense for women (especially for those who earn high salaries themselves) to hinge their marital hopes on meeting Mr. "Big Bucks."

I've lived too long to overlook the obvious reality that we all need money to live, and that the more we have the easier life is. But we don't need as much as we think in order to experience the "good life," and we certainly don't have to expect him to earn it all. Single women who are serious about husband hunting need to start thinking in terms of *combined* incomes. To show you what I mean, let's pretend that you're a woman who earns $50,000 and you meet a great guy who earns $30,000. You like him a lot, but you've considered throwing him over because he's not "successful" enough. Just as you're ready to say "sayonara," it dawns on you that together you have a combined earning power of $80,000. That's the figure that counts! What difference does it make who draws the bigger salary? None.

How the two of you handle the financial disparity, however, is a matter of some consequence. Our society equates money with power, and that equation permeates our thinking. It creeps into our marriages as well. When there is income inequality between spouses, effort must be expended to avoid damaging power struggles. Many women whose husbands earn the lion's share of the family income complain that their husbands treat them as underlings. Women who earn more than their spouses may be tempted to make the same mistake. As long as you are aware of this danger, and willing to work in order to avoid it, you have nothing to fear. On the contrary, you have a better chance of choosing a mate for *who* he is rather than for what he earns. By refusing to be dazzled by the illusory glamour of the success trap, you are more likely to find a mate than all those women who are still waiting for their six-figure dream men to appear! There is no equation between money and happiness if you fall reasonably above the poverty line.

The "Settle for Less" Trap

Some women, especially those who've been unmarried longer than they want to be, begin to get the notion that it's better to be married to anyone than not to be married at all. They lower their expectations drastically, and tol-

erate men who they wouldn't have considered when they
were younger and time was on their side. Some of these
settling-for-less women are the kind who remain in unsatisfying relationships that grind along from month to
month and year to year without any solid base of love,
respect, or real commitment. They stay for convenience,
and in order to feel "coupled" rather than alone. He's
not what she wants, but he's better than nobody.

Others of these women are the type who tolerate ob-
jectionable behavior from men, trading high-quality attention for a lower-quality brand, and rationalizing that
they are lucky to be attended to at all. Still other women
in this trap settle for, and often marry, men who are far
beneath them in every way—intellectually, financially,
ethically, and emotionally. All of the above women share
a common delusion: the belief that to have reasonable
expectations of men is the same as having expectations
that are too high, and that women armed with expectations are doomed to singledom. For them, "settling" is
the same as "compromising," but in fact the two words
have different meanings. To compromise is to bend one's
position a little without sacrificing basic integrity,
whereas to settle is to bend so much that integrity has
to be sacrificed. Women must *compromise* their standard
of the ideal man in order to find a husband, because no
man will fit perfectly into the mold, but they don't have
to (and shouldn't) *settle* for someone who falls so far short
of that ideal that he bears no resemblance to the Mr.
Right they've been envisioning (unless, of course, the
ideal is the mythical knight in shining armor!).

There's nothing wrong with having an image of Mr.
Right—even an idealized one—as long as you can: 1)
compromise when a man comes along who doesn't fit
every specification in your image, and 2) remember that
there is more than one candidate for the position. Although some psychological experts might disagree with
me, I believe that "imaging" serves a useful purpose in
helping women to find mates. When women can form a

mental sketch of a Mr. Right-for-me, it gives them a clear incentive—a goal to attain. Thinking back over my own personal biography, I recall that it was not until I had developed an image of the kind of husband I wanted that I was able to shift from floundering aimlessly around in a romantic sea to keeping myself on a charted course headed for a specific destination.

The "I Can Change Him" Trap

I won't go into detail about this trap because I've discussed it in an earlier chapter, but it bears repeating because it trips up many a woman.

The "I can change him" trap differs only slightly from the "settle for less" trap. If you enter into a serious relationship with a man bent on changing him, you are categorically settling for less except in one instance, which I will explain momentarily. The subtle feature of the "I can change him" trap is that you are unaware that you are "settling." You are a true believer in the "love conquers all" myth, and you are oblivious to the fact that love doesn't *conquer* anything. Love enriches but it doesn't *rehabilitate*. Marriage is an ineffective institutional treatment center. You can't change him nor can your love bring his transformation about.

Sometimes it happens, though, that a man is marvelous in every way except for one flaw. He might be a workaholic, an underachiever, or too tied to his mother, to name a few possibilities. Here again, the same principle applies: *You* can't correct *his* flaw, but you could decide that you are willing to live with it. Recently I read a newspaper article about a famous heart surgeon who is a self-confessed workaholic. In discussing his marriage with the interviewer, he stated that his wife had entered into the union with the clear understanding that his work would always come first. Although she was not interviewed, and might have contradicted her husband's positive view of their marriage, the inference was

that she married with her "eyes open." Using her case
as an example, I'd say that if you know in advance that
you can't expect to change the flaw and you are willing
to accept him as he is, go ahead—with my blessing!
You're making a *conscious* choice which then enables
you to compromise rather than to entertain the devas-
tating fantasy that you will change him. I won't accuse
you of "settling," either, because I will assume that you've
decided that there are enough rewards inherent in your
union to offset the flaw. Let's make no bones about it,
the "reward" is frequently a financial one. Many women
(and I'm not implying that the heart surgeon's wife is
one of them) care a great deal about material comfort.
They are willing to make substantial "trade-offs" for the
benefits of living on "Luxury Street." If you're one of
them, be honest with yourself about it, and determine
in advance what "flaws" you are willing to barter for
financial well-being. One thing is certain, when you accept a man with a major flaw, it's a virtual guarantee
that you'll be expecting compensation in some form.
Make sure you know what you're expecting and whether
or not you're going to get it before you pass "Go"!

Back to Daddy Again, and Lest We Neglect Mommy...

I've already gone on record as an avowed member in
good standing of the "It-all-goes-back-to-Daddy" club,
and I've said that women who get caught in one or more
of the above traps can find their way out by examining
that crucial, primary relationship. The essential tasks
for you are:

1. To identify the areas of deepest frustration, dis-
    appointment, and fantasied idealization in that re-
    lationship.
2. To discover your own trap(s), which is tantamount
    to asking: a) How are you playing out that old tape
    with Dad in your adult relationships with men? b)

What are your *covert expectations* of men? c) How are you expecting to be *paid back* for what Daddy didn't give you? In this discovery phase, I recommend as reading aids: Nir and Maslin's *Loving Men for All the Right Reasons*, Cowan and Kinder's *Smart Women, Foolish Choices*, Viscott's *The Viscott Method*.

3. To move from discovery to *corrective action*. You can't succumb to blaming Dad for the rest of your life, because that prevents you from taking responsibility for your behavior. In the final analysis, you are the captain of your own romantic ship, and only you can decide the direction that it takes.

While it is true that in matters of romance, I think, a Back-to-Daddy expedition yields more significant data than a Back-to-Mommy trip, I don't want to overlook her. Mothers serve as models for their daughters. They provide a one-way mirror through which girls observe female-male relationships over a long time span. The way Mom interacts with the men in her life is either the way daughter learns to do it, or the way she learns how *not* to do it. She can profit from Mom's successes and her failures in relation to men. Of course, it's much easier for the daughter in her own love life if Mom was a positive role model, but it's not necessarily calamitous if she wasn't. Other female models abound in the persona of teachers, relatives, and peers, and the young girl can learn as much from her observations of them. Furthermore, adolescence itself provides societal sanction to acquire newer, more modern attitudes and behaviors toward the opposite sex. Norms for relationships between the sexes change rapidly with each new generation. Lessons taught by Mom are often too outdated for her adolescent daughter. Find me a mother who doesn't hear regularly from her teen-aged daughter: "Oh, Mom, you're so old-fashioned!" The criticism always carries some validity.

I think it's important to review your past relationship

with Mom to determine whether her influence still represents heavy emotional baggage for you in connection
to men, but I believe that in most instances it is easier
to alter whatever later ill effects in relation to men were
derived from a daughter's relationship with her mother
than from her relationship with dear old Dad! I confess
that the evidence for this position is more intuitive than
factual, but it comes from many years of observing
women and from the collection of histories stored in my
memory bank. Then, there is the factor of my experience
as a *female* therapist. Mine differs from my male colleagues' experience with their female clients in one important respect. Female clients can and do use female
therapists as role models in their relationships with men,
and the rub-off effect is often amazingly swift. I take
maximum advantage of that edge in my work with
women by sharing those pieces of my own story that
seem worthy of emulation. Likewise, I get the extra bonus of enhancing my own love life by borrowing from
clients' biographies. Woman-to-woman interaction is
often fairer than woman-to-man.

Here endeth the sabotage seminar. We'll go next to
the sweeter subject of success!

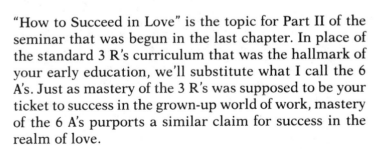
Six Ways to Make the Search Pay Off

"How to Succeed in Love" is the topic for Part II of the seminar that was begun in the last chapter. In place of the standard 3 R's curriculum that was the hallmark of your early education, we'll substitute what I call the 6 A's. Just as mastery of the 3 R's was supposed to be your ticket to success in the grown-up world of work, mastery of the 6 A's purports a similar claim for success in the realm of love.

1. *Attitude:* Clinical psychologist Judith Sills says that "attitude" is the most important factor in determining whether or not you will choose a mate

successfully.* No one who has spent time listening to single people would dispute her. Your willingness to acknowledge and appreciate men's positive qualities can spell the difference between success and failure in your relationships. This doesn't mean that you should ignore the negatives, romanticize them, or pretend that they don't exist, but it does mean that you approach each new encounter with the conviction that almost every man will have some appealing qualities. The aura of enthusiasm that then surrounds you tends to engender favorable responses. Rare is the man whose best foot doesn't come forward when he's with a woman who validates his bright side. Once his credits have been noted, it remains a question of mutual compatibility instead of a grueling exercise in defamation from which you emerge empty handed. So, many women start off on the wrong attitudinal foot. They look *first* at what they *don't like* about men. "I didn't go out with him because he was 40 and I'm 32, and I want someone closer to my age." "We didn't hit it off because I kept thinking, he's overweight 10 pounds or so, and I want someone who's physically fit." In these examples, the initial attitude is so fixed on the negative that there's no room for the positive to emerge. It's over before there's been a chance to begin!

To show you how significant attitudes can be, let's reverse the above statements to give them a different connotation. "Even though I'd prefer to marry a man who is in his early 30s like I am, I went out with Tom, who's 40, because he seemed very nice and appeared to be young at heart." Or "He was slightly overweight, but attractive nonetheless. I liked his sense of humor, so I thought,

---

* Judith Sills, Ph.D., *How to Stop Looking for Someone Perfect and Find Someone to Love* (New York: St. Martin's Press, 1984), p. 171.

'why not give it a whirl even though he probably doesn't jog every day like I do?'" Now, it's a ball-game! Both men are in the batting order. The negatives have been noted, but the two women have chosen to move forward on the basis of their acknowledgment of the positives. Once the pluses have been mentally recorded, an opportunity is created. In the final analysis, these women may very well conclude that eight years' difference in age or a little extra flab are not of sufficient negative magnitude to take precedence over the positive qualities each man possesses. But it is the *attitude change* that creates the *opportunity* to make the final decision.

Attitudes can be insidiously prejudicial or refreshingly open-minded. They exert a powerful influence on important decisions. You can close the door on your chances for loving relationships by establishing silly, attitudinal criteria about men themselves, the kind of work they do, the activities they enjoy, the way they appear, the amount of money they make, or you can *look for* and *look at* the good side of men, and approach the unfamiliar professional, recreational sides of their lives with curiosity and flexibility. Some women are so instinctively talented at door closings that they're unaware of it. If they're lucky, someone will alert them to this debilitating habit. Otherwise, they remain their own worst enemies.

2. *Availability:* In Chapter 3, I discussed the concept of availability as it relates to men, and I emphasized that unavailable men are not worthy of your time or attention. Likewise, you are not a good candidate for marriage if you are unavailable. Women demonstrate their unavailability in both similar and different ways than men do. The most common symptoms of unavailability in women are:

a. Repeated attachments to unavailable men, otherwise unsuitable men, or more than one man simultaneously.

b. Adhering so rigidly to a mental shopping list for Mr. Right that if he doesn't have every attribute on the list, he can't be considered.

c. Allowing work to be all-consuming.

d. Indulgence in flirtation as a means to conquer, break hearts, and then move on.

e. Repeatedly running away from men who are genuinely interested.

f. Refusing to overcome excessive shyness.

g. Gaining weight and keeping it on, or overindulging in other self-destructive habits.

h. Ignoring your physical appearance altogether.

i. Maintaining symbiotic ties to original family such that their values rather than yours are dominant and interfere with your ability to be autonomous and independent.

j. Appearing so desperate for love that everyone is driven away: "I'm nobody without a man."

k. Much ado about "me" and not enough about "you."

l. Physical and emotional "rigidity" or "tightness."

If you're available, you're *open* to new experiences and ideas, and to intimacy itself. You're expressive about your needs, feelings, thoughts, and vulnerabilities, and you're amenable to being known and knowing a man. You can give, and you can receive as easily as you give. Your head is planted firmly above your shoulders, and you use it in your best interests, which include all matters pertaining to the heart. You renounce self-deception. You're enthusiastic about growing. In short, you like yourself and you think other people will like you, too.

3. *Accessibility:*   Before you decide that you've passed the availability test, make sure you also pass the accessibility test. If you're truly available, you're

accessible. A single woman in the city who stays home every night is as inaccessible as her counterpart who resides in some remote locality where there aren't any bachelors. Accessible women are those who plant themselves in places where men can see and meet them. They notice and are noticed, without concocting embarrassing public displays in restaurants, theaters, libraries, offices, supermarkets, and all manner of respectable public and private spaces.

A while ago I was asked to conduct a class for single men and women called "How to Meet Someone of the Opposite Sex in a Supermarket." It was a high point for me and the group. Because we were televised, we attracted maximal attention from customers. The market was selected because of its location in a part of Boston where single people reside in large numbers. With or without a TV crew in tow, that night was tailor-made for the female students. There were men galore! The women (and for that matter the men) who weren't intimidated by the TV cameras came away with names and phone numbers! Those who didn't, couldn't avoid having an osmotic seed planted in their heads. I knew that from then on they would all pay more attention to their fellow grocery consumers! Experience is a great teacher and the best students are *accessible* to new people and new experiences. This particular teacher came away from her experience determined to conduct many more classes in supermarkets!

4. *Assertiveness:* Available, accessible women are assertive. They express themselves in action. They have social skills. Experience has taught them when and how to approach and how to be approachable.

a. *Approaching*

Before you can approach a new man effectively, *you have to divest yourself of any expectations about*

*the encounter. You need to tell yourself that your ro-
mantic fate doesn't hinge on what happens.* You are
only talking to him on the slim chance that he *might*
be interesting. If he responds in your favor, that's a
plus that you didn't expect. If he doesn't, it's not a
strike against you. Once you notice someone or are
aware that you're being noticed, you take advantage
of it. You approach or let yourself be approached.
I said approach—*not attack*—and there is a difference. Approaches are *friendly*: "Excuse me,
where did you find that Chinese tea I see in your
cart?" Attacks are *invasive*: "Hi, that's a great-
looking suit you're wearing. Let's go out for a drink."

Too many women approach men wearing *hope* on
their sleeves. This makes them appear unduly ner-
vous and awkward, and heightens the possibility
that men will respond in kind. Worse still, it takes
the fun out of it. Approaching is flirting, and flirting
is a game. Like all games, it has the suspense factor
of winning and losing. You play because you enjoy
the game. For years, I've been losing at tennis more
often than I've been winning, but I still love to play!
So you need to think of approaching men as no more
significant than a playful activity. Good, wholesome,
adult recreation. To have fun at it you need to be
friendly, relaxed, light-hearted, and a good sport.

Some women never approach men. They want to
be approached, and if they aren't, they assume there's
no one out there for them. All I have to say to them
is, "You don't know how much fun you're missing."
For single women, a little "light" flirting can be the
best game in town, that is, if they understand that
there's a difference between "safe" flirtation and the
"dangerous" kind. The former is interpreted by men
as a friendly overture in which *sexuality* is an
understatement; the latter a sexual overture in which
friendliness is an understatement. When women
overstate their sexuality, they're courting danger.

Most men are as quick to receive sexual cues as they are to initiate or respond to them. If sexuality is on parade, it sets the stage for what proceeds thereafter—SEX. If women want men to take them seriously as human beings, it's poor practice to engage in sexual advertising or activity right away. Flirtation, despite its recreational component, carries some responsibility, the responsibility to maintain a friendly posture (garnished with a "hint" of sexuality) and the responsibility to be clear about what you *don't want* when you first meet someone. If the women I meet are typical of the female single population in general, then the overwhelming majority of them *don't want* to be instant bedmates, but at least half of them wind up being just that and only that. The opportunistic sexual character of men cannot be blamed for all the undesirable "bedding" that occurs. Much of it is related to feminine hopes; the hope for intimacy, the hope that this man will be the one, the hope that the way to a man's heart will be found through his body and yours!

b. *Conversing*

Friendly, amiable conversation is a much safer, more rewarding method of making contact with men. If you like each other as people, the sexual side of yourselves emerges of its own accord. You don't have to *do* anything about it other than looking your best. It's much harder to be a good conversationalist than it is to be sexy. For a lot of people, talking is difficult. Marriage counselors are accustomed to hearing couples refer to "communication problems" as their primary reason for seeking help. Whether married or single, men and women apparently find it hard to talk to one another. Instead of delving into the probable causes of communication difficulties (which are beyond the scope of this book), I will list those attributes that appear to me to be the most essential for good communication:

- *Eye contact*—Looking directly at whomever you're talking to.
- *Openness*—The willingness to reveal yourself: feelings, thoughts, values, attitudes, interests, talents, etc.
- *Directness*—The willingness to verbalize exactly what's on your mind rather than beating around the bush, especially about "delicate" matters such as sex, complex feelings about someone, one's personal inadequacies or vulnerabilities, etc.
- *Curiosity*—The demonstration of genuine interest in another person's life, i.e., his work, activities, idiosyncracies, social perspectives.
- *Humor*—The demonstration of an appreciation for fun, and for enjoying the bright side of life.
- *Enthusiasm*—The projection of yourself as someone who *likes* living as opposed to someone who is *burdened* by it.
- *Empathy*—The willingness to step into someone else's shoes and see the world from his vantage point, and then to respond to what you see.
- *Timing*—Expressing yourself when someone is *ready* to hear you.
- *Listening*—The willingness to hear what someone has to say to you, and to respond to it in accordance with the intended meaning.
- *Cooperation*—The demonstration of cooperativeness rather than combativeness. In conversation, it's avoiding the desire to be "right" about everything.
- *Good manners*—No rude interruptions, tedious monologues, derogatory comments, injurious sarcasms, needless omissions of "thank you" and "please."

c.   *Creating happenings*
     You're out in the world, you're approaching, you're conversing, and at this point, you may well be asking, "Is it all up to women?" "Don't men have to do anything?" The answer is a definite "yes." They have to do all the things that you've been advised to do,

and a little more. Courtship is not dead. Men still do the lion's share of the pursuing, and most women still want it that way.

It's the *first act* of the courtship drama that has been changing so much in recent years. Life is hectic. Romantic opportunities easily slip by for lack of time. It's much easier to go unnoticed now than it was a generation ago, not only for all the reasons I've mentioned previously, but because time is so scarce and men and women are very busy. That's why I, along with other spokespeople on this subject, keep reminding women that it's not in their best interests to sit back and wait for those first overtures to come to them. Scarce moments have to be seized and opportunities created within limited time frames. "We may never meet again if we don't meet right now" is a good motto to stamp indelibly on your brain. For women approaching or already into middle age, the "motto" becomes a "must."

5. *Affection:* Maybe I'm old-fashioned (my teen-age daughter would say so!) but I still think that the ability to give affection is women's strongest suit with men. Lest this should sound deceptively simple, let me explain how I would describe an "affectionate" woman. She has *natural warmth.* She cares *about* a man and what happens to him without having to mother him. She *delights* in him, and lets him know it. She is *continuously discovering him* as a best friend would do. She's unpretentious in his presence. She's *supportive* and *understanding* when he's deserving, but not when he isn't. She *smiles,* she *laughs,* she *cries.* She *angers* when she has the right. She's *demonstrative* emotionally and physically and there's an equilibrium between her sexual behavior and her feelings.

Affection is precious and very scarce these days, despite the fact that sexual activity is rampant among us. Sex and affection make good bedfellows only if we refrain from deluding ourselves into the belief that they are one and the same. Being "good in bed" is not a substitute for being "affectionate." To be affectionate requires the development of the character traits just mentioned, whereas sexual *performance*, if considered by itself, is akin to the acquisition of a motor capability like riding a bicycle. First you ride with your hands and feet firmly planted in designated places, then, with a little practice, you graduate to riding with no hands and your feet on the handlebars!

6. *Assessment:*   To be successful in love, you need to be competent at assessing character, and so I repeat again that simply listening to the cravings from your heart yields insufficient information. Think of assessing a man the way you might judge the quality of a pie at a baking contest, but please remember that the man-assessment is a much more serious matter! If you pay close attention to the signals from your taste buds, you can identify the unique ingredients and evaluate the blend. Assessing male character is comparable to refined tasting. You need to:

a. *Observe behavior.* The way men *act* publicly and privately provides clues to character. Is the behavior appropriate, consistent, and in keeping with promises and words?

b. *Look below the surface.* Even though behavior gives clues, it doesn't always supply answers. There's a difference between *behavior* and *intent.* Examples: 1) A man can *appear* very attentive and solicitous, but have no intention of a commitment. Other clues will be available to demonstrate his lack of commitment but they may not be readily observable on the surface. 2) Good manners can easily be mistaken for affection and kindness, but manners are skin-deep whereas affection and kindness run much deeper. Outward gestures, like good manners, are not necessarily indicative of affection and kindness.

c.   *Ask questions.* 1) Don't make assumptions about men without checking them out directly. Example: Woman says to herself, "I think he's probably scared of his feelings for me." She shouldn't surmise, she should ask. 2) Find out about his past work history, romantic history, and his childhood history. Usually, the tenor of a person's past life is carried over to the present. 3) Ask what problems he has had, and how he's resolved them. 4) Get the lowdown on him, but don't do it like a detective, lawyer, or psychologist would.

d.   *Avoid wearing rose-colored glasses or other blinders.* See what there is to see and when you see something you don't want to see, be sure to look at it carefully. If it looks negative, face it squarely before it's too late.

e.   *Hold auditions.* A male friend of mine, finding himself single in mid-life, made it a practice to hold what he dubbed biannual "auditions" for prospective mates. When he told his friends, he did so in jest, but many of us scurried around to find dates for him nonetheless. Now, several years later, I look back at his experience from a more serious perspective than I did at the time. The concept can be useful. Some people learn best from comparisons. If it's easier for you to discover a man's merits by measuring him against other samples, then do so, but don't let the decision process drag on endlessly. Remember that men are sensitive, too. If you discern that one or more of the men you are dating is seriously interested in you, be straightforward. Let him know where he stands in your esteem. (This sampling method can be an especially useful assessment strategy for women who haven't dated much or for those who married young and divorced after several years of matrimony.)

f. *Be practical.* It's possible to meet men for whom you feel a great deal of admiration, but with whom you just can't roll the dice to your advantage. Here's an example: If you're 25 and he's 45, and you want babies and he's adamant against them, and he has a heart condition, clearly it's not promising, so better to move on despite your feelings for him.

g. *Think.*

. . . . .

The seminar is over. You've been returned to your places in the field. Before long, presuming you've been "good" journeywomen, there should be some "serious" activity on your love screen! The next chapter will help you integrate it. It's my farewell gift to you; you might call it a "love kit"!

CHAPTER 9

How Do I Know When I've Found Him?

"Love is not a feeling," but rather an action or an activity, says M. Scott Peck,* and on this final leg of our journey we would do well to heed his words. He reminds his readers that there is a difference between cathecting and loving. When we *cathect* to something or someone, we are declaring that an object or person is attractive to us, but we can decathect as quickly, if not always as easily, as we cathect. The process of cathecting does not require the inclusion of the activity of loving as a component.

---

* M. Scott Peck, M.D., *The Road Less Traveled* (New York: Touchstone Books, 1978), pp. 116–120.

Love goes beyond cathexis and can exist with or without it. It is a willful decision, a thoughtful choice to behave in a *loving* manner toward another person. Between a man and a woman, it's a commitment to actively nurture the partner's spiritual growth whether one *feels* like it or not. By contrast, there are many instances in which a person can *feel* cathected to someone but chooses not to love him or her. A married woman can meet an attractive man and choose to confine her loving to her husband, thereby excluding the new man. Our individual supplies of love are limited. There's not enough to give to everyone to whom we feel cathected. In addition, but no less important, is the fact that *saying* we love someone is insufficient. It's what we *do* over time, not what we *say we will do*, that counts in love, since all manner of destructive behavior can occur under the pseudonym of "love."

So let's presume that you've done your homework and have participated actively in the field; you've weeded out the Mr. Wrongs, and lo and behold you've come upon a certain someone. Is he the one? How do you know it's right? Remember, love is not a feeling, but a thoughtful decision about a *commitment to be loving*. In effect, you are making a *major* decision, perhaps the most important one you'll make in your life, a decision of such magnitude that you can't afford to leave it to your emotions. What you need is an extensive checklist of criteria to guide you to your decision. Here it is! If you and he pass this test, you can be 99 and 44/100% sure that you've found him!

Him

1. Does he have *any* of the characteristics of the Mr. Wrongs outlined in Chapter 3?

YES   NO

___   ___

   If yes, which ones?_____

   Does he show any evidence of remedying them

   without my interference?_____

2. Is his lifestyle a responsible one and reasonably compatible with yours?

YES   NO

   Responsible a. ___   ___

   Compatible b. ___   ___

   If no, how is it incompatible and does the

   discrepancy violate an important value

   for you?_____

3. Is he committed to you?

YES___   NO___

Evidence_____

_____

4. Is he *actively* and *consistently loving* toward you?

                         YES___   NO___

5. Does he keep his promises to you?

                         YES___   NO___

6. Is he an independent, self-reliant, emotionally

   stable human being?

                         YES___   NO___

7. Is he open, direct and kind in his communication

   with you verbally and sexually?

                         YES___   NO___

8. Do you respect and admire him?

                         YES___   NO___

9. Does he make his needs known?

YES___ NO___

10. Do you genuinely enjoy his company?

YES___ NO___

11. Does he derive satisfaction and self-worth from

his work?

YES___ NO___

Except for the first three questions, all of the above should be answered with an unequivocal "yes." The first question should be answered "no," but I'm allowing you a little leeway just in case he's remedied some of the Mr. Wrong characteristics or exhibits a *relatively minor* by-product of one of them. Question 2 should be answered "yes," in part a, but there is room for maneuvering in part b. An example might be meeting someone whose work necessitates frequent traveling out of town. You would then have to evaluate how his absences would affect you (assuming he's committed to the job). The third question requires an unequivocal "yes," like the remaining questions, and the affirmative answer is so crucial that you need to make sure that you've got plenty of convincing evidence to support it.

You

1. Are you using him in any way to compensate for your deficiencies?

YES__ NO__

2. Are you mistaking any of the following for genuine love?

   a. Dependency—yours on him

   YES__ NO__

   b. Chemistry—are you overemphasizing the sparks between you?

   YES__ NO__

   c. His prestige and success

   YES__ NO__

d. His dependency on you

YES___ NO___

e. His need to use you as a therapist rather

than a spouse

YES___ NO___

3. Go back over the preceding "Him" list and

substitute *you* for him. Example: Am *I*

committed to him?

YES___ NO___

All the answers to questions 1 and 2 should be unequivocally "no." Question 3 should be tabulated as explained in the "Him" section; in the yes or no slots, fill in the total number in each column. Once again, a reminder that there are positive and negative answers to these questions. In order to get maximum benefit from the checklist, however, you must respond honestly. No cheating. The "wrong" answers are your red flags— they're meant to warn you about potential danger. They should prevent you from moving posthaste into matrimony. The relationship may or may not be lost, depending on the quality and quantity of red flags, but certainly their existence will require corrective action *before the union takes place.*

Corrective Action

Psychotherapy is the prevailing American form of corrective action. Like love, effective therapy requires a commitment from the client to participate actively and to tolerate the temporary discomforts that change entails. In all my experience as a therapist with couples and individuals, I've never seen a client change unless he or she desired to for his or her own sake. If a woman tells me that she is visiting me at someone else's request, I want to know first whether or not she would have been propelled to come under her own steam. If the answer is "no," and it often is, she is sent packing until she is moved by her own spirit to be present. For a "committed" client, the advantages of psychotherapy over other forms of "help" are compelling. Good therapists have the benefit of third-party objectivity combined with an understanding of the complexities of human behavior. Once the therapist makes a commitment to help someone, he or she is as honor-bound to the client as the client is to the therapy.

Love

It is paradoxical that, having recommended psychotherapy as the best strategy for corrective action in matters of love, I cannot recall much, if any, direct discussion about love in my professional training. With the benefit of hindsight, it appears now that my teachers danced rather skillfully around the word. To the extent that we were exposed to the debris that came in the wake of love gone wrong, we were protected from learning about how it could go right. Certainly, we were never called upon to explore its meaning, much less put it into practice. If we happened to read Erich Fromm's *The Art of Loving,** it was because it was "au courant" rather than required! It wasn't until Leo Buscaglia came along that love got a foothold in the university classroom and from there into the vast public study halls opened up by television and lecture tours.

One man cannot do the work for all of us. It's up to us to carry the banner. *Love is the bottom line.* Without love, we don't fare very well in life, nor do our children, and eventually whole societies suffer the consequences.

So what is love? Please understand that in attempting to answer the question, I don't claim expertise. Much of what I know about it has been gleaned from listening to people's stories and experiences, and from reading the works of wiser mortals than I. The rest of my knowledge comes from my own personal trials, tribulations, and triumphs in the name of love! I am still learning about it. It is the nature of love to supply as many questions as answers. So, from a humble calling place, I define it here with the accompanying caveat that the definition is necessarily incomplete.

Love is *energy*—a force that energizes the lover and loved one alike. It moves us, challenges us, and fosters our growth. It encourages self-actualization as much as it encourages togetherness. It's dynamic and thus ever-changing in mood, intensity, and character.

Love is *communicating and listening*. It is *expression*—open, honest, and direct—and it is hearing and validating what has been heard.

Love is a *process*, like a stone that gathers moss as it ages, in contrast to a prize that one wins, displays, occasionally remembers, and just as soon forgets.

Love is *commitment, attention, compassion*—the commitment to be there for someone, the attention to the effort that must be expended to keep the commitment,

* Erich Fromm, *The Art of Loving* (New York: Bantam Books, 1956).

and the compassion to accept and understand the imperfect but beloved person.

Love is *fun*. You "click" with each other, amuse one another, and the ways that you do it are both familiar and new, and the potential to draw on your joint fun account is ever-present. You delight in each other. Fun is the secret language that you perfect over the years.

Love is *pain*—the *shared* pain of disappointment, failure, hardship, growth, illness, tragedy, and death.

Love is *peaceful*. It is the synthesizer that blends the world sounds and assures that every loved one plays an instrument in the orchestra.

Love is *creative*. It seeks and finds new expressions and discards worn-out ones. Instead of being a creature of habit, it is a creation wrought from dynamic imagination.

Love is sometimes *crazy*. It gives you permission to intermittently lose your way, your emotions, and your control, but never your freedom.

Now, it should be obvious that a dilemma has been posed. Suppose you passed the check-list test with flying colors and arrived at the love definition. How can you be sure that love is what you've got right now when I've just said that it's a process that evolves over time? First, you need to understand that if you think of love as a "forever" phenomenon, then you can't be sure, but if you think of it as "now," "forever will take care of itself," to quote Leo Buscaglia.* Loving *now* is like establishing one of those popular retirement accounts. With each passing week, month, or year, you invest in the account. Someday, when it matures, you can anticipate a handsome return on your investment. Meanwhile, you get enjoyment from watching it grow, and you take personal pride in having had the discipline to maintain it. The maturity day is so far away that the gratification you

---

* Leo Buscaglia, *Loving Each Other* (Thorofare, N.J.: Slack, Inc., 1984), p. 150.

will derive from receiving your pot of gold is more a figment of imagination than of immediate reality. Your pleasure is in the building of the account, not in the receipt of the pot of gold. So it is with "now" love. You keep investing in it and delighting in its growth, and you forget about the pot of gold. It's when it has totally vanished from your mind that you're most likely to receive it.

Second, you need to give preeminence to that much-maligned word "commitment." As I've already explained, the concept of commitment took a beating in the '60s and '70s.

To many young people in those days, marital commitment represented entrapment, like being committed to prison or a mental institution. It was true that the older generation often *behaved* as if they were "locked into" matrimony—unwilling victims, as it were. The distortion of perception lay in the assumption that it was the *commitment* that caused the *imprisonment*, when in actuality, the *lack* of genuine commitment was a more likely cause. Commitment, in the context of marriage, should be a fully conscious, willful, heartfelt choice to devote oneself to loving someone. The committed couple then are *choosing* active participation over passive submission. Seen from this perspective, commitment is a decision about behavior. I love, therefore I will behave in a loving way, and if I'm not committed to loving, there can be no love.

Frequently, people speak of commitment as if it was the same as fidelity, but there's a difference. Fidelity is a part of commitment—not the whole of it. Marriage partners may *contract* with one another to be monogamous, but fidelity is not, in and of itself, evidence that a true commitment exists. Commitment requires much more effort than the simple adherence to a vow of fidelity, but fidelity certainly enhances the prospects for a relationship to succeed. Thus, it is a major component of commitment. There is no question in my mind that a spouse who enters into extramarital affairs is putting his or her primary commitment in jeopardy. Sometimes the damage is irreparable, but not always. There are instances in which the *temporary* meandering of one or both partners serves to put them on a stronger course with one another. Still, it's high-risk activity that doesn't warrant encouragement. Since experience is probably the best preparation for marriage, one of the strongest arguments against young marriages (roughly from 19 to mid to late 20s) is that the participants are often so inexperienced in dealing with the complexities of human behavior and interaction that infidelity is almost predictable. No wonder they stray from the marital nest! They want to learn what they don't know about people, especially about the opposite sex, but they forget that there are propitious times for acquiring knowledge. Marriage is not the university of choice for a sophomoric student of human behavior! Singledom is! Put experience under your belt *before* you take on a responsible job. Some of you will whiz through your training; others will need more time. Be sure to take the time you need. You'll be rewarded in the end.

· · · · ·

We've come to the end of our adventure together— the place where we part company. Of course, my parting wish for all of you is that when you are asked how much you enjoyed this imaginary trip, you will be able to respond in earnest: "It was fruitful."

EPILOGUE

Five Women Tell Their Stories

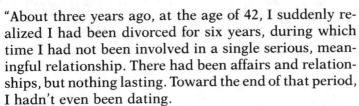

"About three years ago, at the age of 42, I suddenly realized I had been divorced for six years, during which time I had not been involved in a single serious, meaningful relationship. There had been affairs and relationships, but nothing lasting. Toward the end of that period, I hadn't even been dating.

"I decided it was time to change the situation, but how? And how could it be different? Why had I been in relationships that either didn't work out or just went nowhere? What was my role in the direction my life had taken, as far as men were concerned? How did one go about finding someone who wouldn't disappear after a few dates, or leave the relationship when the going got rough?

"Coincidentally, I received a flyer describing a number of courses, one of which was called Spouse-Hunting. It sounded perfect and I signed up immediately.

"There were six of us: five women and one man. Besides providing some comfort in that others were in the same situation, the course answered a lot of questions, taught me things I hadn't known, and opened new doors. And it was fun!

"I learned three very important things: First, that the sexy, attractive, elusive men to whom I had always been attracted are the least likely to make commitments. Secondly, 'Love is half head and half heart.' Thirdly, there is absolutely nothing wrong in deciding what you want in a man and going after it in a systematic fashion.

"Armed with these three tenets, I proceeded to implement my learning and joined a dating service, first making a list of my criteria (that in itself is a learning experience). I ruled out the elusive, charismatic types and proceeded with a much more open mind.

"I quickly learned that no one meets all of one's criteria and more soul searching took place as I revised my priorities.

"I met a man who did not meet my original standards for culture, income, and education. He did possess human qualities I had never thought of as essential to a good relationship, i.e., sense of humor, warmth, integrity, and unconditional acceptance. Making a relationship work was as important to him as it was to me.

We now live together in a relationship to which we are both committed. I believe this can be attributed to the courage I gained from Spouse-Hunting, courage that enabled me to look at myself, open my mind, and look at men and relationships from a new perspective."

. . . . .

"I was 43 years old and had been divorced for 15 years when I met my husband on a blind date arranged by a mutual friend. It was not love at first sight, so the relationship was a friendship for the first six months. We got to know each other gradually, without the intensity of a sexual affair. When we finally realized that we were in love, we had a solid base of respect and compatibility.

"During the 15 years I was single, I had numerous affairs with married men, younger men, and men who had no interest in making a commitment to me. These affairs were intensely painful and unsatisfying. At 40, I realized I needed help with this problem, and I put myself into a concentrated program to address it. I took the est training and went into therapy. The latter included sessions with my mother and a trip to my father's grave. I read all the self-help books I could find, and kept a journal. It was painful and hard. My only hope was that I could stop being with the wrong men. I did not believe I could ever find the right man.

"When I met my husband, I intuitively knew he was the right kind of man for me, but I felt no 'chemistry.' In fact, the thought of a romantic relationship with him seemed unrealistic and uncomfortable. With the help of my therapist, I was able to tolerate the discomfort and continued seeing him as a friend. Finally, I was able to relax and allow myself to receive the kind of love he was capable of giving.

"It is hard for me to believe that I allowed myself to spend so many years in relationships that were going nowhere and were giving me so little. The key to the change was really working on myself and becoming clear that I wanted and deserved a committed relationship with a strong, capable man. I'm glad I refused to settle for anything less."

. . . . .

"I have recently turned 40 and have never been married. I was raised as an Irish Catholic in the Boston area.

My background brought me problems as a single woman. Ever since adolescence, I had been inundated with parental and sibling demands and expectations. Our household was controlled by a mother who was both status conscious and achievement oriented. She had to approve of whatever I did. I had to date the 'type' of men my mother and brothers would like. My family could be very intimidating to individuals who were suspected of not being 'good enough.'

"I spent many years holding on to different men for security and comfort, knowing well that they did not meet my standards (or my family's) as marriage partners. Also, I had been rejected quite often, and that left tremendous scars and no self-assurance.

"From early adulthood on, I was so sensitive to the social stigma of not dating someone that I determined that I was better off holding on to some companionship than to be left alone. Today, being alone is something I have grown to accept, but only grudgingly.

"After experiencing more rejections and a family tragedy, I chose to pursue individual counseling. My first experience with it was disappointing. I dropped out and continued my life as it was. By the time I reached my late 30s, I chose to pursue counseling again but with someone who specialized in 'relationships.' My goal was to become more introspective and to learn how I picked the 'wrong' men and became involved in dead-end relationships. This time, I found out many things about myself—some happy, some sad. I discovered that I had to change many of my attitudes and prejudices, and work on my inability to cut loose from family and former relationships. Holding on has caused me great pain.

"My therapist suggested a dating service for me—preferably video because I looked good and presented well (so I was told). Well, I did it—why not? I met and dated many very fine men for a period of three to four months until I met a very special individual. On that first date it clicked but only because I allowed myself to look at the person from a new perspective, free of family biases.

"Had I not done so, I would have passed him by, because he did not pass the family litmus test. Our relationship is now growing and is characterized by caring, sharing, and good times. He is committed to me and to working on our relationship.

"I can honestly say that five to six months ago I would have refused to go out with him but my therapy sessions have opened up my attitude, feelings, and heart."

. . . . .

"I am 40 years old. I was married for 16 years. I've been separated for one year and eight months, and my divorce became final just recently. I live in an apartment with my adolescent daughter.

"One of the hardest things about the separation was actually deciding to do it. Even when I realized in my own mind that there was no other way, it took a long time to force the issue and make it happen (I'm basically a passive person). For the longest time, my response to the situation was just to withdraw. I could not, and did not want to try to make things better. I was afraid of the unknown, and had little confidence, so I was stuck.

"Initially, after my husband and I separated, I plunged myself into work and daily routines. I spent a year and a half doing little else—just sometimes going out with a few women friends I knew through work, or seeing my family. I went through some real ups and downs, and the downs were terrible bouts of loneliness, isolation, and pessimism about meeting any man who would really want to know me!

"The two things that helped me to improve my life were a job change and seeing a therapist. I had always worked, but several years ago I got a job where I was able to develop new skills and receive a lot of support and encouragement. I was getting praise and developing confidence there, which I wasn't getting at home. Therapy has been a tremendous help to me in sorting out what I really want (and *am*), and has helped me to make decisions and follow through with them.

"One day my boss told me about a singles group. Although he had told me it was a very welcoming, friendly, nonthreatening group, I was terrified of the whole idea. I went to one function (a forum) a year after the separation, and liked the people I met, but still couldn't bring myself to go regularly.

"About six months later, a woman I had met through my boss (and a member of the group) asked if I'd like to go to one of the dances with her. I did, and had a fair-to-good time. At the same time, on my own steam, I decided to go to an introductory meeting of Parents Without Partners. I actually ventured out to one of their dances totally on my own.

"Although I haven't followed through on PWP, the other singles group has been a real door-opener for me. It's exactly what my boss said it was, and by the third dance, I was looking forward to dancing and socializing—not staring at the floor! It's particularly good to realize that everyone understands what you've been going through and we even talk about it! I'm making new friends with both men and women (the woman who introduced me has become a good friend). It's made a big difference to me just to be going out!

"Just recently, I've started dating, which has been especially nice because that wasn't one of my immediate goals when I first joined the group. I feel lucky to have this particular group, because I understand that singles clubs vary. It's still scary being on my own (with all the responsibilities), but I'm really optimistic about my situation for the first time in a long time, and I feel more 'me' than I've felt in years."

· · · · ·

I would not have had the incentive to teach classes or write a book on this subject if I hadn't struggled as a single woman. My own romantic odyssey took me through countless relationships with men. Until about the age of 29, I allowed the prevailing winds from the heart to guide me wherever they would. Usually, they left me shipwrecked. Like the other women in this chapter, I turned to therapy to correct my course. There, I finally learned that I could control my own romantic destiny.

The first therapeutic lesson was lengthy and difficult. It involved the reliving of my personal history and the rediscovery of forgotten memories of early losses, the sum of which was a full-blown case of commitment-phobia. For years, I had deceived myself into believing that all my dating experience represented an earnest search for a husband. I ignored the fact that I had a better-than-average ability to become attached to *unavailable* men.

The second therapeutic lesson was shorter and easier. I learned how to *discard* after a few dates rather than put myself through an entangled, fruitless affair. I ruled out all men who:

- however charming, involved me in *triangular* arrangements with mothers, ex-girlfriends, ex-wives, current wives, or employers
- suffered from alcohol, drug, or serious mental health problems
- were *unavailable*—the elusive types (there were many)
- were dishonest, over-achieving, dull; who intellectualized at the expense of sensitivity; who had uninteresting work and friendship networks, or who had dissonant political, social, and psychological values

At the same time that I was discarding, I was adding new men to the pool through friends, parties, dating services, jobs, and chance encounters.

The final therapeutic lesson required patience and relaxation on the husband-hunting front and considerable effort on other fronts. Through the aforementioned process of elimination, I learned much more about my image of Mr. Right. I knew the character of the person I was seeking. To help the process along, I rid myself of whatever petty criteria stood in my path, such as demands that he be wealthy, exactly my age, or from the same socioeconomic and ethnic background. To complement these mental gymnastics, I made some changes in my professional circumstances. I changed jobs frequently until I found the perfect one. It had to be one from which I could derive pleasure and to which I could make a significant contribution. This was a calculated decision based on the fact that the majority of my time was spent at work, and so it would be there that the best of myself would be most visible and noticeable. My search for *him* became less self-conscious and more focused.

When I was 32, I met my husband-to-be. He came to work in the same place where I was employed. Later, I could point with pride to having heeded my own best instincts. To this day, I often speak of work and love in the same breath.